GW00566726

THE BEST YEARS
OF FLYING

THE BEST YEARS OF FLYING

Howard Fry

The Book Guild Ltd
Sussex, England

The Book Guild Ltd
25 High Street,
Lewes, Sussex

First published 1999
© Howard Fry, 1999
Set in Times
Typesetting by Keyboard Services, Luton

Printed in Great Britain by
Bookcraft (Bath) Ltd, Avon

A catalogue record for this book is
available from the British Library

ISBN 1 85776 475 7

CONTENTS

1

The RAF's Better than the Dole

It is hard, I expect, for today's fortunate young to understand that when I left school in 1930 it was just a dream of unattainable bliss to go to university. True, my form-master at St Paul's did say that he thought I might be worth a university course. But both my father, a middlingly successful professional singer, and my grandfather, the works' director of a small explosives company, told me firmly that a university training was a waste of time and money, and it was time I got a job.

With millions out of work, getting a job was quite a trick in 1930. And really about the only way was to make use of any kind of personal contacts you might have.

Naturally, I did everything I could to find work. I applied to the big banks and insurance companies and to the oil companies, but competition was keen and I achieved nothing. True, my Matriculation Certificate, reasonable school reports and my tolerable record as an oarsman did get me one or two interviews with such prestigious firms as British Petroleum and the Hong Kong and Shanghai Bank. But in the end the job was not mine.

Then, I saw a little advertisement in the paper. 'Young men with good technical education wanted' it said 'as pilots in the Royal Air Force'. And I duly filled in the coupon and applied for the job.

And at last came some luck. I had applied to the RAF for a Short Service Commission and naturally told my mother about it. To my great good fortune she remembered that Colonel Illingworth, a friend of hers, knew someone high up in the Air Ministry.

He in turn was one of the people who served on the Selection Board for new Pilot-Officers for the RAF. So it was only natural that I got all the hints and tips as to how to succeed when I came before the Board.

First of all I was told, 'Be very early.' If you turn up on time, well, you are pretty late! 'So try ten minutes early!' Then you must be dressed in the right way, well-polished black or brown shoes, and definitely no suedes or co-respondent shoes, as two-colour affairs were known in those days. As to suits, I was warned against a sports coat and flannels. 'Wear a sober grey suit,' I was told, 'with a plain white shirt and an old-school tie'. Then there was the question of a newspaper. 'You cannot possibly turn up with the *Express* or the *Mail*,' I was told, so I played safe and had the *Telegraph* under my arm. Even then I was told, 'Be sure you have read the editorial and know what it was about!'

Then Colonel Illingworth was careful to tell me about the interview itself. 'You may as well get it right!' he said, and told me that 'Why do you want to join the Air Force?' and 'Are you ready to serve abroad?' were two of the main questions. The replies they expected were: 'Sir, I have always wanted to learn to fly,' and 'Sir, I have always wanted to see something of our great Empire!'

When the great day came it was almost a pushover. There I was a good five minutes early ('God help those who were even one second late'). On my head was a neat bowler hat ('pork-pie wearers, if they did but know it, were wasting their time'). My suit and my dark tie were sober, my white shirt and my black shoes shone with brightness; and I noted with glee the number of other applicants wearing startling country tweeds and even, horror of horrors, suede shoes. I went in for my interview with the *Telegraph* under my arm having carefully read that day's editorial, happy in the knowledge that the poor

2

fellows waiting with the *Express*, open at the sports page, might just as well not wait at all.

I gave the expected replies and I passed the interview. The other candidates I met at the interview I never saw again! I think they must have come with the wrong newspapers!

I do not know with what sort of emotions young men would now join the Air Force as Trainee Pilots. But I can tell you that in 1932 the whole thing was enormously exciting. Flying then was something for a tiny privileged few; that I would be paid the princely sum of eleven shillings (55p) a day while I was being taught to be a Pilot struck me as amazing; and I was even rather pleased at the prospect of wearing the rather odd RAF uniform of those days, which consisted of a very tight waisted jacket of light Air Force blue, worn with riding breeches, puttees and highly polished boots. The whole was topped off with an exceedingly hard uniform cap and one had to carry both a walking stick and brown leather gloves.

Although the Air Force provided the money they warned us that going to a cheap tailor was pretty risky! 'If we don't like the uniform when we inspect it then you'll have to get another one at your expense.' At the risk of seeming to be a man who played safe, I have to confess that I had my uniform made by Fulcher of Savile Row. Naturally, I had no trouble getting it approved and there was even no adverse comment on my very colourful mess-kit and my impressive great-coat.

It was in this rather amazing rig that we young hopefuls started our Air Force service at the Drill and Disciplinary Centre at Uxbridge. Although this little course of only three weeks was very short, it remains indelibly in my memory. There were the long hours of square-bashing with Sergeant Major Nightingirl bawling: 'An Officer is an Officer, an Airman is an Airman, and you see before you a Warrant Officer, First Class, of the Royal Air Force. But as for you lot – Acting Pilot-Officers on Probation – you are the lowest form of life in the Air Force.' In case we were in any doubt about who we were and how we stood he made that clear too.

3

'When you are here on parade, you call me Sir! And if I should meet you in uniform on the camp, I call you Sir! The difference is – you mean it! Now for God's sake, pick your feet up and try to march like men, because the married quarter we are now passing belongs to Mrs Nightingirl, and if you cannot do better than this I shall never hear the end of it. Very well then, we'll try double-marching!'

So although it was a hot August day we burst into a run. Not long afterwards Acting Pilot-Officer Carden collapsed in a faint. All the Sergeant Major said was, 'Pick up that rubbish you two men and lay it on the grass! He'll be better when he has had a rest.' And he was. There were, of course, sessions of PT (Physical Training) and boxing during our three weeks at Uxbridge. The Sergeant Major took a close interest in boxing too, and a typical comment was, 'Hit each other harder or by golly I'll get in the ring and knock you both out!'

And finally, after we'd learnt to march, to shoot a bit, to box enough to keep the Sergeant at bay, came the great day when we had jumped the first and lowest hurdle. We were now accepted enough to be sent to the wilds of Lincolnshire, to Number 2 Flying Training School at Digby. But before reporting there we discovered something new about the Air Force. This was that life really did not have to be so earnest and concentrated as it had been in our civilian jobs. After a mere three weeks or so in the Service we found that, wonder of wonders, we were allowed a week's leave.

The RAF Station at Digby was quite a change from the rather armyish atmosphere of Uxbridge. The main business here was flying and the starchy discipline of Uxbridge was greatly relaxed. We put our breeches and boots away for ceremonial occasions and wore slacks and shoes instead. We discovered that the staff of the training school were very human, reasonable people. Although we had to call them all 'Sir' (young men were not nearly so rebellious as they have now become) we always spoke of them using their nicknames. The Officer Commanding was Group Captain 'Crasher' Smith, so called because he was unusually accident-prone. The Chief Ground Instructor was Squadron Leader 'Happy' Horrocks.

My Flight Commander's name was Restell-Littell; so he was naturally always known as 'Bide-a-wee'.

Horrocks earned his nickname because of his habit of wearing a high smile whatever he had to say to you, for example: 'Bad luck laddie, you are no damn good and you'll never make a pilot.' Or perhaps, 'Try a lot harder lad, or you will get your bowler hat (the sack). Remember there are plenty more where you came from!'

As to Crasher Smith, we were soon to learn how he got his name. We had only been at Digby for a few weeks when one of our pupils crashed his 504 in the forced-landing field. 'Bloody young fool,' said Crasher. Later he crashed beside the pupil! And was he in deep trouble? Not really! You see, in those days Group Captains were very important people and as to Avro 504s, they were only made of steel tubes and linen covering. So the Groupie's rigger just put everything straight again and nothing was said.

I learnt to fly in the wood, wire and fabric of an Avro 504. First used in the Great War, by the 1930s it had been brought up to date a bit and had quite a reliable radial engine called a Lynx. But, of course, there were no brakes, no electric starter and the compass was decidedly dodgy. With all its faults and primitive equipment I still think the 504 was a first-class training plane and probably much more instructive than the easier, safer machines in use today.

Luckily, nowadays, aircraft engines are very reliable but in the early Thirties they might stop any time. So one of the most important things to learn was how to make a forced-landing. I was practising this one afternoon and I got lost; it is funny to think of it now but I just went back to Digby by rail! First of all I found a train (easy to spot because of its plume of smoke); then I flew over the nearest station to find out where we were; and then I followed the railway route back to base. Flying Officer McCulloch was, surprisingly, quite pleased. As my instructor he was waiting for me to fly back. 'You're not such a bloody fool as I took you for!' was all he said.

Bide-a-wee was my Flight Commander and a very quiet, reasonable man he was, as well as being meticulously careful and conscientious. The RAF training of those days was very thorough and it took me 14 hours over three-and-a-half weeks before I finally went solo.

'You're no born natural pilot, Fry,' said Bide-a-wee at the end of the last period of instruction he gave me, 'but you're not like some of these bloody young fools. So off you go. You probably won't kill yourself.'

Whatever else you do or don't achieve in life, the moment when you first fly an aeroplane on your own always lives in your memory. I still remember the careful adjustment of the safety harness and the goggles, both absolutely essential in those days when you sat in the open air and the propeller directed a gale of engine-heated air over you before you even left the ground. I remember taxiing, ever so slowly, to just the right point on the big grass field so that I could get a good long take-off run right into the wind; the careful run-up of the engine; and then the big moment easing the throttle open, keeping the machine straight with rudder and opposite stick, rocking forward to get speed up and at last the gentle pull-back to unstick from the ground.

'You've done it now,' said the sombre voice of reason. 'One thing to get up here,' as the ground slid away fast below, 'but the trick is to get down.'

And, in truth, there is a moment of panic when you wonder whether, without the instructor, you can do a decent safe landing. But a few minutes of thought, of telling yourself that you have landed lots of times, dual, and you start the approach. I don't believe mine was the smoothest landing done on a first solo, but it certainly was not the roughest. And taxiing in I certainly did feel very elated, understandable perhaps in an age when pilots were pretty rare and strange people.

To some extent the rest of the year-long flying course was an anti-climax. I learned how to do simple pilot-navigation, how to do loops and slow rolls and in my senior term how to fly an ugly duckling of a plane called an Armstrong Whitworth Atlas. And, of course, in the classroom there were lessons on discipline, King's Regulations, Air Legislation and the theory of how aeroplanes are flown and navigated.

A few highlights stick in my mind. The haunting notes of the Last Post, and the sharp crack of the rifles as we paid our last respects to the two pilots killed during the training year; the delight when a policeman in pursuit of a speeding pupil-pilot was caught on the camp and put in the Guard Room for the night; and not least, the mistake of trying to buck the system: pupils were a bit rebellious about doing exercises on the parade ground on a cold winter morning, and we very unwisely asked the PT Sergeant whether it was really necessary. The next morning we appeared as usual in our vests and shorts whilst he came in a truck and wearing his thick uniform and a great coat. 'Right-ho my lucky lads,' he said, 'you get on the truck and we are going to drive you five miles out into the country. Then I'm going back for breakfast. If you want any you'll have to run damn fast! Remember it finishes at 8.30!' Needless to say we did not argue any more.

Of course we got into trouble of various sorts. Someone was caught with the Chief Flying Instructor's niece in his bedroom. And, amongst others, I was carpeted for drinking too much beer. Happy Horrocks, although he smiled throughout the interview, was terse and effective: 'Fry, the Mess Sergeant, tells me you had eight pints between dinner and closing time last night. If I drink that much I get stinking drunk. You must therefore have been disgracefully drunk too. The Mess Sergeant has been told not to serve you with any alcohol for the rest of the term. Dismiss.'

But despite all the difficulties, and after around 150 flying hours apiece, we received our coveted wings and passed out as fully fledged Pilot-Officers, no longer on probation. All of us that is except for poor Rhys-Jones, the Welsh vicar's son, who, it was claimed, just could not fly well enough, and the cheerful character, whose name escapes me, who got 'ploughed' for beating up the passenger vessel, *Skegness Queen*.

The sort of squadron you went to depended on how you had made out at Flying Training School. The few bright boys, like Hugh Le Good and Horace Darley for example, who were thought to be born pilots, went on Fighters. But pedestrian characters like myself were sent to Night Bombers. But I can't say I shed any tears over it. I still reckoned life was great. I had a secure job for the next five years at least. I had a car. My old school mate, Barbara, was willing to go away for a weekend with me now and again. And, above all, I was an intrepid birdman, a pilot in an age when there were very few of us.

Then my posting came through to No 58 Night Bomber Squadron, flying the funny old 90 mph Vickers Virginia, and based very pleasantly at Worthy Down Aerodrome near Winchester. There I went with great contentment in August 1933. No worries, you might ask, about going to war in anything so antediluvian? Quite honestly, I did not think a war was very likely. Britain in the Thirties was still a first-class power with a huge Commonwealth at her beck and call. And it seemed to me that nobody was going to be silly enough to attack her.

Few ways of life could be more comfortable and genial than the Air Force between the wars. Once I had passed my training all the pressure was off. I no longer had the anxiety of passing the course, getting off probation and so on. And Worthy Down was just the place to settle down to the business of being a peace-time Junior Officer. The camp was oldish and mellow and the mess even had quite a pleasant architectural style about it, with good food, comfortable rooms and not bad furniture. The Station Commander was Group Captain A A B Thompson, a very socially-minded man with a pretty wife, who liked arranging all sorts of functions to keep us Junior Officers out of mischief. There were frequent parties of one sort or another at the Group Captain's married quarter, a very large civilian-looking house away from the camp on the outskirts of Winchester. The Groupie's wife had a long list of healthy, respectable, young ladies, who were judged 'suitable' for us. But her normal geniality was apt to evaporate if some young officer, greatly daring, produced his own girlfriend, who was judged to be not quite a lady.

The Air Force were now concerned with making some use of us. We had to start off as Second Pilots (Day); travel quickly through the position of First Pilots (Day); reach the exalted rank of First Pilot (Night) and finally become Night

Instructors. The fact that rank really had nothing to do with it was shown by the fact that the very experienced Flight Sergeant McCreery was 58 Squadron's Chief Night Flying Instructor. I was assigned to him and he soon had me flying the ancient Vickers Virginias around the small grass field at Worthy Down. What sort of plane was the old Virginia? Well, to those who have not read their history books from those days, I can tell you that the Virginia could fly at a stately 90 mph but, unfortunately for its pilots, it had open cockpits and could stay in the air until you were frozen stiff after eight hours. How did we even keep warm enough to land after a long night flight? It's all a matter of your clothes. And really, we were just like Biggles! We wore our blue uniforms of course and over them we wore silk undersuits. And then we topped this with leather-fleece-lined Sidcot suits. On our heads we had lined leather helmets and our hands were protected with silk under-gloves and fleece-lined gauntlets and on our feet we had fleece-lined leather boots.

Parallel with the life as an RAF pilot was the equally important life as an Air Force Officer. We new young Officers had a Squadron Leader assigned to us. He told us when to wear our ordinary blue uniforms, when to put on the more official tunic and riding breeches and when to go the whole hog with the very smart mess-kit. Then there was the business of 'calling'. You have to call on both the Wing Commanders and their wives, we were told, and then you must call on all four Squadron Leaders and later on you should call on the Flight Lieutenants in your squadron who have married quarters. 'Calling' had its own routines. First of all, you wore a decent suit; then you gave the batman who answered the door your visiting card; and finally, if your hostess asked you in, you had just one drink and then left. We were told, 'There's no need to call on Flight Lieutenant and Mrs Harrison – they do not have a married quarter'. So young men being what they are, we called on the Harrisons just the same. And they were very pleased to see us. 'We could have had a quarter,' Leela Harrison told us, 'but life on the camp is horrible, the Wingco wives are always telling you what to do.'

9

But the Group Captain's wife was a very different person.

'You must not call on Mrs Thompson,' our Squadron Leader told us, 'she is a former actress and she does not like that sort of thing. She will ring you up when she's ready.' And certainly Mrs Thompson was one of her own! A very positive lady! I did not have to wait long before she rang me.

'Is that Fry?' she asked, and got straight down to business. 'Fry,' she asked, 'have you got a girlfriend?'

'Well, no, Mrs Thompson. You see, I've only just arrived.'

'Never mind, Fry. You can have Valerie. She's a Brigadier's daughter. I know her quite well and she's coming to my moonlight picnic on Sunday. You'd better come too. By the way the men bring the drinks and the girls bring the food. Val knows the form. OK? Well, goodbye Fry. See you Sunday.' And indeed the moonlight picnic was good fun. The Group Captain came and brought his wind-up gramophone and some decent records. Valerie? Well, she turned out to be quite a pleasant girl. But she did not like the situation much.

'It's all very well of Mrs T,' she complained, 'but I don't know you and you don't know me and how on earth does Mrs T know we'll get on together?'

We simply put up with her bossy ways. And in truth, Val and I got on quite well together. I suppose that, looking back at things, one of her great advantages (unusual in those days) was that she had a car. It was a very small Austin Seven carefully labelled 'Pity Me'.

'I say, Val,' I asked her, 'why is your little car called Pity Me?'

'It's all you damn great Air Force Officers!' she said. 'You weigh the poor little thing down!' And I suppose that in the old days my weight of $13\frac{1}{2}$ stone was fairly heavy.

The peace-time Air Force was naturally keen on sport. All of us played squash regularly on the camp's excellent court and then there was some not too ferocious sparring in the gym. The camp had no facilities for my sport of rowing but my records must have shown somewhere that I had done cross-country running, so the following episode took place not long after I reached Worthy Down.

I was summoned from the 'flights', as the Flight Offices near the hangars were called, by the usual distressingly smart airman from Station Headquarters.

'Pilot Officer Fry,' he intoned with a superior smile, 'the Group Captain wants to see you – immediately.'

So off I sped to the great man's office, pausing to ask if the adjutant had any idea what it was all about.

'Not a clue, old lad,' he replied, and as there had been no response to my knocking on the Group Captain's door, he added, 'I'd just barge in and salute him if I were you.'

But the great man still made no sign even when I saluted with the then usual click of the heels. After a few moments I tried, 'Good morning, Sir.' But nothing happened. At last he looked up.

'Who are you?' he asked.

'Pilot Officer Fry, 58 Squadron.'

'Ah yes, Fry. You're Officer in Charge of Cross-Country Running.'

Now this was not the case so I ventured a firm, 'No Sir.'

'Don't you argue with me, Fry,' came the swift reply. 'If I say you are Officer in Charge of Cross-Country Running then that is what you damn well are. Is that clear?'

'Yes Sir.'

'Alright then. Go to the Station Warrant Officer's office and he will put you in touch with the NCO in charge ... and one more thing, Fry.'

'Sir?'

'The Officer in Charge never comes in last. That's all.'

Back in the world of flying I was soon a Night Captain and judged suitable for the eight-hour flight to Birmingham and the long, boring criss-crossing for the local searchlights. But one of the disadvantages of becoming more experienced was that you became suitable for flying with your Wing Commander! One night they said, 'Well, Fry, you can go around the searchlights with the boss man.' And off I went with Wing Commander Oswald Modin. Life is often just luck and one of our two Napier Lions played up. So the Wing Commander decided to land at Farnborough and let the engineers have a

11

look at it. Unfortunately, Wing Commanders did not do much flying and you could say our Wingco was a bit out of practice. Anyway, unfortunately, he dropped the old Virgin and damaged the undercarriage. So we spent the night in the Guard Room in Farnborough and we had to go back to Worthy Down in a couple of cars!

But the fact is that at Worthy Down we did very little flying. The expansion of the RAF had not yet got under way and the general word was to the effect that we should not be spending too much money. So in 12 months at Worthy Down I only did 200 hours flying.

The Virginia, like the first plane I flew, the Avro 504, was a survival from the Great War. It was a massive bi-plane, made of metal tubing with fabric covered wings, and like the Avro it had an open cockpit. Here the two pilots, clad in their Biggles outfits, wrestled with the big heavy controls. In a little cabin behind them was the wireless operator, while in the nose was the navigator/nose gunner. Way down the tail, on his own, was the tail gunner. My Virgin flying was mostly cold and boring, though one incident does stand out in my mind.

I am sorry to say it occurred not long after my first solo flight at night. As young pilots will, I started to imagine I was pretty good and I took to cutting my approaches nice and short to avoid the long taxi back for the next take-off. But like a damn fool I overdid it and nipped the top off three small trees. On today's all-metal machines nothing much would have happened, but in a Virgin all the fabric was torn and I had to taxi ignominiously to the tarmac. Was I court-martialled for careless flying? No, the Thirties were easy-going days. All I got was a gentlemanly rocket from Group Captain Thompson and a more vigorous and colourful one from Flight Sergeant McCleery and all was forgotten. The aircraft? They repaired it without too much trouble.

I suppose the greatest pleasure in it for me was to go through the various stages of becoming an efficient night pilot and navigator and finally being approved as a night-rated Captain. Sure it was cold and boring but there was some satisfaction in flying from Winchester to Bristol, on to Hull, back to bomb a target on Salisbury plain and back home in the wee small hours to eggs, bacon and coffee in the mess.

Unfortunately, all good things come to an end eventually and the sad day dawned when 58 Squadron was moved to Upper Heyford near Oxford. Frankly, we all hated the place. The CO, whose name I have mercifully forgotten, was very unlike our Group Captain at Worthy Down. He had no interest whatever in throwing parties but a lot of interest in forcing pilots on colour-hoisting parade at 8am even when they had been flying all night. His wife was a canon's daughter, so church parades were many and had to be well attended. The social life was also grim with quite a lot of impossibly snobbish dances in the Mess, from which we were often excluded, or excluded ourselves, because we did not fancy meeting the ghastly Army types or Hunt members.

There were already two Hart (day bomber) squadrons there and the station was not at all tuned to our night-flying ways. I fell out with the Station very soon. Not long after we all went to Heyford our Wing Commander scheduled some night flying throughout one Saturday night and of course I was part of the programme. In the old Worthy Down days none of the night pilots were ever put on Sunday church parades. So I did not even notice that I was supposed to appear in my best blue at 9am on Sunday morning. Later the same day, having made up my lost sleep, I was walking across the parade ground and a very loud voice said, 'Mr Fry, Sir, can I have a word with you?' It was the Station Sergeant Major and he wanted to know why I had not obeyed Station Standing Orders.

'Oh,' I ventured, 'we never go on church parade if we have been night flying!'

'That will not do, Mr Fry. I shall tell the Group Captain and he will not be pleased.' And he certainly was not!

'You must understand, Fry, that the Station Sergeant Major runs this Station for me. As for you, you are just another Flying Officer and I don't want any more trouble with you.'

Life at Upper Heyford was rather disagreeable in other ways too. The local police pursued our men for every conceivable fault, such as having tyres without enough tread or lights which were not bright enough. But perhaps we did not help friendly relations when we reported a local Constable for coming on the camp without permission. He did not enjoy spending the night in the Guard Room! Of course, from Heyford the local town was Oxford and young Air Force Officers were often mistaken for undergraduates. Being pursued by 'bulldogs' who demanded to know 'your name and college, Sir?' becomes a bore after a bit.

It was at about this time that something happened which was to set the pattern for my future life. I was chosen, to my considerable pleasure, to fly out to India, as second pilot and navigator on a Vickers Valentia Troop Carrier Aircraft. The Valentia, though a bi-plane like the old Virginia, was a much more modern and much faster machine. And the trip itself gave me the chance to see a bit of the world, and in particular a bit of the British Empire. Perhaps I should interject here that although I had always been a Liberal, far from feeling ashamed of the Empire I was rather proud of the achievements of the British pioneers, who had created it.

Really, the trip out to India was enormous fun. We took it very easily indeed with night-stops at Paris, where we were very well received, and Naples, where, on Mussolini's orders, we got the cold shoulder. In contrast, we got a splendid reception in Tripoli. Over the drinks and the banquet in the Italian Air Force Mess, we were firmly told that it was General Balbo who called the tune in Libya. Whether the rest of the trip was technically through Empire countries or not, every airport seemed very British and very efficient. Although Egypt, Iraq and India were certainly hot, the RAF Messes in which we stayed were comfortable and well run, with good food and plenty of the cold drinks we needed. Finally, all of 12 days after we had left England, we arrived at Drigh Road RAF Station outside Karachi.

But the real turning point in my life was the flight back to England on Imperial Airways. The aircraft was the huge glistening Handley Page 42, a massive four-engined machine which was by far the biggest aeroplane I had ever seen. Back in those days it was all first-class. The seats were very

14

comfortable, the food and service superb, and of course there were cold beers and chilled wine to help the journey along. The only thing the dear old 42 did not have was speed – it did about 95 mph.

Perhaps this would be a good moment to say that for some time I doubted whether I really wanted to try for a permanent commission in the RAF. Although it was a good lotus-eating existence you did rather ask yourself what you were achieving. And I, for one, could not help remembering what Flight Lieutenant Harrison's very sweet little wife said to us bachelors one day.

'Well boys, if you do have plans to get married sometime get out of the Air Force first. Whether you live on the camp or off it's just impossible for those below the rank of Squadron Leader. Of course, in the married patch you get a quarter for almost nothing, but then you are bossed up and organised by the Wing Commanders and their wives. And if you live on your own, like Harry and I, well, all you can afford is a ropey flat like this and Cyprus Sherry.'

So when Captain John Harrington (known as 'Jovial Jack') invited me to the cockpit and stated baldly: 'Cut above Service flying isn't it, old boy?' I could not disagree with him. There he was in a big, comfortable, closed-in cockpit, with no need for a helmet, flying suit and gloves. When his lunch was ready a polite steward would let him know and he would go back to eat it in the huge passenger cabin. At night stops he would have the best room in the hotel. And added to that his pay was the enormous sum for those days of £1,000 a year.

The effect of all this magnificence, plus the obvious efficiency of the Imperial Airways ground stations, made up my mind for me. I would, I decided, try to get into Imperial, although I realised that it was going to be quite a grind to get the civil pilot's and navigator's licences which were absolutely essential.

Life at Upper Heyford continued to be grim indeed after our happy days at Worthy Down. The only interest for me was that the Government of the day had at last woken up to the menace from the Axis Powers and had started to expand the Air Force.

15

The method was fairly simple. Each flight of a squadron was expanded into a squadron on its own. Thus 'B' Flight of 58 Squadron, in which I had served since leaving Training School was suddenly made into a new Squadron, No 215. This naturally meant that we split ourselves into two flights and took on a lot of new pilots who had to be trained. I was pretty busy on this training work. And at least we had a hope on the horizon. The expansion meant bringing a lot of old Great War aerodromes back into use and we hoped fervently that 215 Squadron would soon be posted to one of these new Stations.

But before any of this could happen I had some good luck. The RAF, with the next war in mind, wanted to train some specialised navigators. They were beginning to realise that the fairly simple pilot navigation in use in the Thirties would not do for the faster, longer-range aircraft that were coming through. So each bomber squadron was told to get at least one Officer trained in navigation. Realising that the syllabus for the RAF course was very similar to that for the Civil Navigator's Licence I lobbied my CO hard in order to get the first vacancy on the RAF Navigation Course at RAF Manston. And in January 1936 I was off to Manston to make a start.

In those days not everything, by any means, was really efficient in the RAF, but the navigation courses were really good and extremely concentrated. We did about 20 hours per month of navigation, mostly in a rather engaging little amphibian aircraft called a Saro Cloud, and all the rest of the time we were hard at it in the classroom. It is interesting that quite a lot of people reckoned that a navigation course was one way of making progress in aviation. At Manston with me at the time was Lieutenant Heimstra of the South African Air Force, later to be Chief of the South African General Staff, and Vin Glasheen of the Australian Air Force who had a good career in BOAC. As I said, after the easy old ways of a peace-time squadron, it was a tough course, but I passed reasonably well and promptly took the extra subjects for the Second Class Civil Air Navigator's Licence.

When I got back to Upper Heyford in the spring I found that the pace of RAF expansion was quickening. Although only a

Flying Officer I was now Flight Commander of 'B' Flight 215 Squadron with a hell of a lot of training to do both by day and by night. Another group of people who were stepping up their activities were the searchlight boys and we spent many a cold night on exercises with them. The great idea of course was to get right over some big city like Birmingham without the lights finding you. But they quickly got pretty good at finding you and you sat up there in a blaze of light reflecting how easily you could be shot down.

At the end of the summer, to our great delight, we got away from the starchy, snobbish atmosphere of Upper Heyford and moved our whole Squadron to Driffield in Yorkshire. This RAF Station, in the East Riding between York and Bridlington proved to be a very happy spot for us all. Admittedly, we lived in wooden huts and, to start with, had no proper hangars for the aircraft, but the good Yorkshire folk around soon made us feel really welcome. And instead of wasting time on parades we were able to get down to plenty of solid flying training and practice.

All the omens were right from the start at Driffield. As soon as the Station opened the local Chief of Police called on the Group Captain and said there would be none of the victimisation of young pilots which seemed quite a feature of police activity in some parts of England at that time.

'Any small matter like Air Force people having a few drinks too many or perhaps speeding a bit in their cars, I'll just turn over to you,' he told the Groupie. Relations with the police were always good.

The Chairman of the local council threw an excellent party for the RAF and we all met the people living around. A friend of mine, Darb Welland, and I were sitting listening to the band when a lady came up to speak to us.

'Are you men on your own?' she asked and told us that her son was a Flying Officer, who, although he could not come to the party, had urged her to come along and meet some of us. So here she was and she introduced us to her daughters and invited us to Sunday lunch. It was a splendid start to life at Driffield, especially as Joan Stickney and her sister became

17

our new respectable girlfriends, for taking to Hunt balls and Mess dances. Perhaps I should remind you that in the rather strait-laced Thirties your partner for big functions had to be very respectable; and you could not possibly take your local 'floosie' if you had one.

Another great advantage of a night-bomber station like Driffield was that we did not have any nonsense about putting pilots on early morning parades. We just got on with the job of getting plenty of flying practice. For example, every year we flew off to the RAF station at Aldergrove in Northern Ireland for a sort of Summer Camp, during which we dropped practice bombs at targets in Lough Neagh. There were also sessions of target practice for our gunners, who banged away at targets towed past the plane.

Even in the Thirties there was trouble with the IRA. Four of us were driving back from Belfast to Aldergrove one night when one of the men in the back seat of our car shouted, 'Stop for God's sake!' We stopped the car and looked back and there were two RUC Constables with rifles trained on the car.

'Just as well you stopped when you did!' they said. 'Another minute and we'd have drilled you full of holes!' It appeared that the IRA had just raided a Belfast Post Office and stolen some money. And it was bad luck for us that they had been driving the same sort of car.

I had another piece of good luck in those days. The Air Force decided that all experienced pilots ought to have Instrument Ratings. So as I was then Acting Flight Lieutenant I had to fly around in the Group Captain's Moth, with the great man's safety pilot, and in the fullness of time I flew down to Hendon and passed my instrument rating. The RAF were nothing if not helpful. If I filled in a form I could get a Civilian Pilot's Licence and I duly did this.

By then it was 1936 and it was obvious that to go to war in a Virginia would be absolute madness. So we were getting rid of the old girls. In theory we were re-equipped with the Handley Page Harrow but as usual they were somewhat behind time. So 215 Squadron was given some Ansons to tide them over until the Harrows arrived.

18

In these days when speeds of 500 mph are quite usual it is strange to think of how slowly we flew in 1936. We had six Ansons then and they cruised at 145 mph, although after the Virginia's 90 mph we thought the Anson was quite a good plane. But its bomb load was very poor so we gradually changed to the Harrow. Although I think the German Air Force would have laughed at it, it did have a cruising speed of 170 mph and several modern features – we had no worries about using it in the smallish grass aerodromes of the Thirties. For example, although the undercarriage was fixed it was well faired, and the flaps good for a short take-off. There were quite adequate landing lights for night use. Then there was an enclosed, hydraulically-operated gun turret front and rear.

By this time I was Chief Night Instructor and I was kept quite busy training pilots on the Harrow. And for about six months I was Flight Commander because we were waiting for a Squadron Leader. This was good fun really, though actually in many ways a flight is run by the Flight Sergeant. In those days he was called the Chief and was a senior and experienced engineer. But he was pretty useful when you were trying some man for a misdemeanor. He knew everyone and had their record taped. For example, if some man was late back from leave the Chief would know if he did this habitually or whether it was just a one-off case!

In 215 Squadron we were getting pretty good at formatting the Harrows. Perhaps we were too good! Because when 213 Squadron at Feltwell had a ghastly accident and flew three Harrows into each other they called in 215 to restore their morale. So, Flight Sergeant Williams, Flight Sergeant Adams and I were posted off to Feltwell. And really things over there were pretty bad. Six pilots had been killed as well as around ten ground staff. And the rest of the Squadron were convinced that the Harrow was just a bad plane and difficult to fly in formation. So morale was rock bottom. When we arrived we could not even get three aircraft out on to the tarmac. And although we eventually got them we had to threaten that the local Flight Sergeant would be put on a charge unless serviceable planes appeared. We tried approaching the Wing

Commander and the two Flight Commanders but their morale had dropped to zero. So for some days we flew the three Harrows in formation over Feltwell using 215 crews. Then gradually we took 213 men with us and finally we managed to get their pilots to sit in the second seat whilst we demonstrated that the Harrow was a perfectly good plane even for formation flying. And success came at last. The 213 people brought out three planes and flew them themselves. So after some weeks we went off back to Driffield. It had been a worrying and tiring task. And there had been no amusing incident to relieve the gloom. Unless, that is, you count my experience when I took the Feltwell church parade. You could ask why I did it anyway. The answer is that the padre wanted a parade and the 213 people were so shell-shocked from the crash that only very junior hands were ready to appear. Now the joke was that having given them the quick-march and marched off ahead of the troops I completely failed to notice that they were all shortish chaps whereas I was just over six foot. Anyway, the upshot was that when I got to the church the troops were quite a long way behind. But luckily Flight Sergeant Williams was alive to the situation and he stepped to the side of the column and ordered, 'Detachment form two deep and enter the church.' So you could say that I 'saved my bacon!'

We got back to Driffield on a Sunday and I had my bad news straight away. When I called at the Stickney house I found that Joan was off and away. Her young sister told me the sad news that whilst I had been away Joan had changed boy-friends to a very wealthy Australian called Lindy Lindemann. His folks were the owners of the big Aussie firm which made Lindemann's wine and sherry. Needless to say, he had a very impressive Alvis car whereas my car was only the cheapest model then on the market, a £100 Ford. But 12-year-olds do not care much about cars and Vera was very cross about her sister's actions.

'I think it's beastly of her,' she said. 'And so does Mummy!' But, as the Americans say, 'You cannot win them all!'

During this period we got rid of our Ansons and had our full

20

complement of Harrows and I gradually moved up the ladder until I was 215 Squadron's Chief Night Flying Instructor, but unfortunately I lost my position as O/C B Flight. You see, Squadron Leader Groom had arrived and, simply, he out-ranked me. But one thing balances another and I had my success in the field of rowing. When I first went to Driffield I had joined York City Rowing Club and as a rowing man from schooldays I had no difficulty in joining their first four. And we gradually improved our rowing until we became Champion Crew of the Ouse. This was I think partly due to the fact that we adopted my school slogan, 'Mileage makes champions'. And whenever we could we used to row up the river to Nunmonkton.

I was doing a Short Service Commission which lasted for six years. So you can appreciate that at the end of five years I was not particularly thinking of finding another job. But once again fate took a hand. By the same post I received two letters. Both were from Air Vice-Marshals – both very senior hands to me. One was from AVM Sir Tom Webb-Bowen and it was very terse and to the point.

'Sir,' it said, 'I see you have Civil Pilot's Licence Number 12622 and Civil Navigator's Licence Number 443. Presumably you would like to fly for this Company [the letter was on Imperial Airways notepaper]. Please sign the enclosed contract where I have indicated and kindly report to Stafford Road Training School at nine o'clock on the 3rd of August 1937.'

The other letter was from the Air Ministry and it said, 'Sir, I understand from AVM Sir Tom Webb-Bowen that he has offered you a position as a First Officer in Imperial Airways. The Air Ministry strongly recommend that you accept this position. You are assured that if you do transfer to Imperial Airways the Royal Air Force will cancel the remaining year of your Short Service Commission and your obligations as a Reserve Air Force Officer.'

You do not get letters of this sort every day, so I went to see my CO at Driffield. To my surprise he was most enthusiastic about the whole idea and he said in his usual fatherly way:

'Well, laddie, you could say that from the observant men of the Air House, nothing is hid. They could see that you were interested in civil flying. Else why would you be getting these licences? So they've made it easy for you. Take my advice, laddie, sign on the dotted line right now. It's a great opportunity. Just ask my adjutant and he'll dope out a good covering letter for you.'

So the die was cast and I was off to Civil Aviation, a very different world, as I was soon to discover.

He then added, 'Congratulations, Fry. I am very pleased for you. Mrs Murlis-Green and I have been talking about all this and we are very sorry to hear that many Short Service Officers have been unable to find decent jobs. You must come along for a drink and tell us about your new job.' This was doubly good news because the Group Captain lived in a very fine barge-conversion on the canal and because Imperials were offering me the then princely sum of £600 a year going up to £1,000 when I became Captain. Both sums were more than RAF pay.

I now had to face my own CO, Wing Commander Sylvester Quine, a very conscientious and rather serious man. He was furious.

'You know, Fry, I think this is disgraceful. You've had the advantage of RAF training as a pilot and a navigator and now you're going to take yourself off to Imperial Airways. I think it's wrong, absolutely wrong. We need you here. I shall try to get you retained in the Service, whatever you say.'

You could see how the Wing Commander felt: he was trying to expand his Squadron and get everyone trained as day and night pilots and navigators; and one of the men he needed was swanning off to civil flying. Whether he did try to stop my departure I have no idea but if so it had no effect and on the 29th July 1937 I did my last Service flying – giving dual instruction on the Harrow to nine different pilots – and had the traditional Guest Night before ending my five years in the Royal Air Force.

2

Sprog Civilian into Boat Mate

You could say that being in any of the Services in peace-time is a kind of protected, insulated life. Not for the lucky young Officer the struggle to find somewhere to live – he has a comfortable, warm room in a Mess. Not for him the restaurant meals at inflated prices – he gets good food at well below the market price. And he gets other 'perks' too, like cheap drinks and laundry and a batman or batwoman to clean his shoes and make his bed.

So when I left No 215 Squadron, RAF, and reported for duty at the Imperial Airways Training School at Croydon, in 1937, it was much more than just a change of job. It was a complete alteration in my way of life. To begin with I suffered a big drop in pay, from £440 a year as a Flight Lieutenant down to £300 a year as Junior Mate, in training. And then I had to find somewhere to live, at a rate I could afford. But Sir Tom Webb-Bowen, the retired Air Vice-Marshal, who was Staff Manager of Imperial Airways, and the man who had recruited me for the airline, was full of optimism about my long-term prospects, and full of advice on dealing with present problems. My first interview with the great man was indeed useful and encouraging, but it had its amusing side too. For Sir Tom had a side-kick called Whittaker, and every pronounce-ment he made to me, was also referred to this complete yes-man assistant.

'Well, Fry, welcome to Imperial Airways. You've got a wonderful opportunity before you. Eh, Whittaker?'

'Yes, Sir Tom.'

'Of course the pay is small now. Three hundred pounds a year isn't it, Whittaker?'

'That's right, Sir Tom.'

'Well, you won't starve on that, eh? But you'll have to find a good bargain as far as digs are concerned.'

'Of course he will, Sir Tom! But we'll give some advice, I expect?'

'That's right, Whittaker. Go to the Airport, Fry. Talk to the traffic boys and girls. They know the ropes, eh Whittaker? Find you something good in the accommodation line.'

'That's right, Sir Tom, put him on his way as it were.'

'Good man, Whittaker. Now look here, Fry, you've got a wonderful career in front of you. Just you listen here.'

Sir Tom went on to tell me about the fleet of four-engined all-metal Empire Flying Boats that Imperial were just introducing into service.

'Fry, these are going to be the finest fleet of transport aircraft in the world, thirty of them, and all capable of carrying twenty-four passengers and a tonne of mail, at one hundred and fifty mph. And you're going to be part of this great enterprise, if you get cracking on this engineering course, and then the seamanship course. You could be a fully qualified Flying Boat First Officer, earning six hundred pounds a year by this time next year. Now what do you say to that, eh?'

'Jolly good, Sir,' I ventured, as friend Whittaker seemed to have fallen silent at last.

'Right then, laddie, cut along and get yourself organised. And if you have any problems come and see me.'

The great British Depression was still around in 1937. So I scarcely needed the Staff Manager's pep talk. I was profoundly grateful not only for my good job, but also for the remarkable prospects it offered. Sir Tom's forecast of £600 a year in a year's time meant I would be earning about four times the average wage at the time, and by the age of 25 at that.

24

The ubiquitous Whittaker had followed me out of Sir Tom's office to expand a bit on the subject of accommodation.

'When you've finished today's lectures, I think you would be wise to talk to some of the traffic people about finding digs. Although we have some addresses ourselves, they are pretty run-of-the-mill places at around twenty-five shillings a week, for tea, bed and breakfast. But you'd want something better, I expect.'

Soon all of us ex-service pilots were in the engine class and meeting Willie Walder, an excellent instructor on engines, who seemed mildly surprised that we had no Engineer's Licences already.

'You'll never get anywhere in this Company without your Ground Engineers' A and C. I imagine most of you want to go on the Empire Boats. And I can tell you now that no First Officer is going to be allowed on them who isn't a properly qualified engineer, able to do straightforward maintenance jobs. And you'll need the Licence, of course, to sign the machine out at the end of each job.'

So the pattern of our days was established. In the mornings we were taught all about the internal combustion engine; how to treat it properly; and how to put it right when it went wrong. The mornings also featured other training for the Airframe Licence. Here we met Henry Calaz, who talked to us about the construction and repair of wings and tail units, the vagaries of flaps and undercarriages and tyres. A nice chap he was, tolerant of our little jokes, one of which sprang from our lessons on the construction of the De Havilland 86 Airliner. Much of this seemed to be constructed of screws, glue and gimp-pins. So this became our catch phase as in the following example:

Calaz: 'Now this morning we'll talk about the under-carriage. It is of course secured to the main spar by . . .'

The class: 'SCREWS, GLUE AND GIMP-PINS.'

And the more absurd it sounded the better we liked it.

Our afternoons were spent in the engine shop, stripping down engines, examining and cleaning them, and building them up again. And in the evenings we went on the night-shift in the hangar, under Bill Budge, the Foreman. Bill was one of the real old school, never seen without his white coat and his bowler hat. He certainly taught us a lot about the night routine maintenance they always carried out, and could sometimes spare time to talk to us about the bigger inspections being carried out on the land-plane fleet of Imperial Airways.

Although the Imperial Airways training was pretty good, the Air Registration Board could scarcely be expected to give new chums like us licences straight away to maintain Short Empire Boats and Bristol Pegasus engines. So the first part of our course was to get a licence for the relatively small, simple DH 86 Landplane and for its motor-car-like engine the Gypsy Six. With this under our belts we would tackle the big stuff.

Naturally, it was not all lessons in the class-room or hard graft in the hangar when I was at Croydon. Now and again I did a bit of flying to keep my hand in. Imperial had a couple of the airliner versions of the Avro Anson and I did a bit of flying on these. They were quite nice to fly but the passenger load was so small that they could not possibly make a profit.

As the engineering training progressed so did the kind of flying I did. Soon I found I was the proud owner of Ground Engineer's Licences for the DH 86, with its Gypsy Six engine. And Imperial thought it was about time I flew this rather unusual little airliner. It had been developed for Railway Air Services and Hillman Airways, as well as Imperial, from the famous Dragon, and its successor the Rapide. These little planes were the first small airliners to be capable of running at a profit, provided, of course, you had high loads and low overheads, and Edward Hillman, the East End bus proprietor certainly had both. The 86, still a bi-plane, but with four engines was the logical development. It carried, as I recall, about 12 passengers and wafted along at a fairly creditable 130 mph. I use the word wafted, because like all wooden machines, it had a very flexible feel about it, and had a slight tendency to wander gently, especially coming into land.

Someone, I am sure, is going to complain that life just cannot have been as serious as I've painted it. Well, they are wrong.

26

Maybe I would have liked to have lived it up a bit more but I had realised that Civil Aviation is not the Air Force. Lighthearted, high-spirited characters were not wanted in my new profession. So like the rest of the boys, I was trying hard to seem the kind of careful, double-check-everything kind of character that Imperial liked. As far as feminine company was concerned, finishing my stint one day I met the girl who was to be my future wife. She was Joan Vivian, an art student from South Africa. I was fascinated by her serene face, excellent figure and dress-sense, and her long hair, which she wore in a classical bun.

About this time, three of us, Townsend, Mulholland and I, decided that we could live better, and more cheaply, by renting a furnished house. A three bedroom 'semi' in Selsdon Park Road, it cost us £2 a week with a further ten shillings (50p)for the lady who came in to 'do for us'. As an Aussie, Mulholland was quite a good cook, and when it was his week cooking we did not fare too badly, but Johnnie Townsend was a terrible cook and when he was doing it I sometimes used to wish I was back at the hotel run by 'Ma' Dendy, an airline traffic officer, where I used to lodge previously. But the big advantage really of the house was that the three of us could swot in the evenings and quiz each other on the mighty flying boat.

We were not at the house very long because Imperial Airways' courses were fairly flexible affairs and they were shortened if the pupils could manage to 'beat the clock', as it were. In the spring of 1938, as the happy holder of Pilot's, Navigator's and now the prescribed Ground Engineer's Licences, I was very pleased to be posted off to Southampton. At last I thought I was getting near the stage when I would get that £600 salary and fly on what was recognised as the world's best airliner.

The first part of the course to give me 'webbed-feet' or make me a member of the 'boat-union', then quite an élite of both service and civil flying, was to teach me something about surface vessels. This meant a short course at a Sailing School, run by a retired Naval Officer, Commander Webb. Here we discovered how to tie and loosen the ropes used to moor vessels up; how to sail a dinghy and a small yacht; how to handle single- and twin-engine launches; and the intricacies of coping with the tides.

At the end of this quite pleasant interlude I was posted to Air Service Training at Hamble aerodrome for my first experience of taking off and landing on water. We flew the tiny little Cutty Sark amphibians, taking them off from the aerodrome, winding the wheels up and then landing on Southampton Water on the hull and floats. And thereby hangs a tale. 'Uncle' Glover, a New Zealander, and I had 'gone solo' on the Cutty Sark and were detailed to get in some practice, taking it in turns to try our hand at landings and take-offs. Uncle had a little Scottish Terrier and we decided that rather than leave the little chap in the car we would take him flying. But being in an aeroplane seemed to upset him and we had quite a job quietening him down while we came in for the first water-landing of the day. As a result we both forgot all about winding the wheels up.

Landing an amphibian on water with the wheels still down is not something I would recommend. One moment Uncle Glover and I were skimming above the surface of the water at 70 mph and the next we were stationary and pointing towards the bottom. Luckily the little plane bobbed back upright with nothing worse than a stalled engine and two neat round holes in the windscreen where our heads had hit it. Then came the silly part of the episode; the engine, naturally, refused to restart, so we decided to try to get a tow back to base from a passing launch or cruiser. There were plenty of these as it was a warm sunny day. But unfortunately, when we waved frantically for help, they all just waved back and thought what a couple of friendly pilots we were. The tide was going out fast, and we had visions of making a land-fall on the Isle of Wight, when the pinnace put out from Hamble at last and towed us in.

The little Cutty Sark was really only useful to give us all some idea of marine aircraft and after a few hours on it, we graduated to the big three-engined Calcutta, which Imperial Airways kept for training. Although much smaller than the C Class boats, this old machine gave us the chance to learn the finer points of flying flying-boats, such as cross wind take-offs and landings. These days few pilots know much about boats so perhaps I should explain that whereas a landplane will generally keep going on the surface, in the direction in which its wheels are pointing, a flying-boat has no desire to go in any particular direction. This means that the pilot has to be very firm and decisive in operating the flying controls, and the throttles on the engines, in order to make the machine go where he wants. You could, I think, sum it up by saying that, although you need more skill and concentration to fly a flying-boat, it will take-off or land with a worse cross-wind than can be accepted with a landplane. And, of course, the boat has two other big advantages: it is perfectly safe for down-wind take-offs and you can also land safely, completely blind.

After some happy days splashing about in the Calcutta, both dual with Captain 'Bill' Bailey, and solo, doing things like anchoring, mooring up and landing in rough seas off the Isle of Wight, I was finally judged to have come to the end of my training and to be ready for a supernumary trip down the route. This was set for 15th July 1938, when I was slated to go as third pilot to Captain 'Ted' Rotheram, down to Durban and back. So at last I had reached my goal: I was a properly qualified First Officer (or Mate, as they expressed it on boats) with Imperial Airways' topline outfit, the Boat Division. And, of course, my pay had gone up to the splendid salary of £12 per week.

Life, I judged, had now become sufficiently promising for me to consider marriage. So I proposed to Joanie Vivian and was very happy to be accepted, especially as her father, Ewart Vivian, Chairman of Holman Brothers (SA) Ltd, the mining machinery people, was, not surprisingly in those days, not too happy about a son-in-law in anything as harum-scarum as civil aviation. Joanie and I saw him off one day at Paddington, in the far-off days of spotless chocolate-and-cream carriages and gleaming green locomotives.

'Howard,' he said, 'why don't you give up this flying business? It's not much of a life. And I'll get you a good job in South Africa.'

'You know, Sir,' I replied, perhaps with more pride than

common sense, 'I've stood on my own feet and earned my own living since I was 19. And I'm not going to let someone else find me a soft job now.'

The train pulled out then and I rather wished I had not been so brusque about it. But I think he respected me for my independence.

To understand my excitement as the day came for my first long trip on a C Class Boat you need to remind yourself of the state of the world of civil flying at the time. Until George Woods-Humphrey, Air Commodore Brackley and the other Imperial Airways' Chiefs had the courage to order the 30 Empire Boats straight off Short Brothers' drawing board, the Imperial Fleet was a pretty motley assortment: 95 mph Handley Page 42s trundled about in Europe and the Near East, 100 mph Kent Flying Boats crossed the Med, and in South Africa and the Far East there were 120 mph Armstrong Atalantas, a little more modern, but with woefully unreliable engines.

Imperial's main competitors were KLM, who flew the latest and fastest Douglas, the DC2 which, although it did 140 mph, was much smaller than the C class boat and had only two engines. In America there was then only the one international carrier, Pan-American, and as a patriotic Briton I was delighted to note that their Sikorski Flying Boat was considerably slower than the Empire Boat. Perhaps I should mention one last thing which made the Imperial Airways Boat Division so special – and that was the All Up Mail Scheme. Under this, letters for any part of the Empire were carried by air, at only three halfpence per letter, or the same as the inland rate.

Taking everything together I was bursting with pride and enthusiasm as, clad for the first time in my dark blue uniform with gold wings and stripes, I reported for duty at Berth 50 in the Southampton Docks area, on that bright July morning.

There is a great advantage in operating a flying boat from a big stretch of water like that at Southampton. This is that there is often no need to taxi around and take-off into wind. Instead, the pilot just points the 'boat' out to sea, gently accelerates and finally takes-off; and this is what we often did at Southampton.

In those days it was rather exciting; as you gradually picked up speed you swept past plenty of great liners and you realised that you were the representative of the future.

The flight across France was often very impressive. We could see the mountains of the Massif Central and the great River Rhône before we landed on a big lake outside Marseilles. The French always do things differently from everyone else and true to form the arrival in Marseilles was rather surprising. As you approached the harbour, a fast launch came whizzing past the 'boat' and threw out a line. Once the Radio Officer (who acted as bow-man) had made this line fast to the bollard in the bows, the coxswain of the launch pointed the flying-boat very accurately at the embarkation point. Then when he was sure it was going to come to rest at exactly the right point the Radio Officer threw off the line from the launch and prepared to secure the line from the quay. It sounds risky and perhaps a bit tricky but it worked very well. There was a large network of ropes coming out from the quay and the 'boat' used to slide gently into this before a big platform with its own ramp up to the quay was lowered into position. Then passengers and crew could come and go as they pleased. The customers (as we called them) and the Captain were served with the usual excellent French coffee. And the rest of us got on with our duties. For the First Officer this meant checking the Shell barge alongside and supervising the refuelling. They were certainly the easy old days! The 'boat' only held 650 gallons (enough for about 450 miles) so we always just filled right up. On the side of the hull there was a single-point fuel connection and the tanks had automatic cut-off valves. The Shell Barge's big diesel engine was used to pump the fuel so the whole business was over in around 15 minutes. Then the First Officer was entitled to report the barge skipper if he took longer than two minutes to come alongside. The same procedure took place at every refuelling stop so the time-table allowed just 30 minutes on the water at each station; and this was, of course, a lot quicker than landplanes of those days.

You have to remember that in 1938 people were used to sea voyages which, for example, took 15 days to Cape Town. So,

31

although Imperial Airways could have scheduled their 'boats' to fly straight through the night, they decided instead to land every night and take their passengers to hotels. This meant, of course, that Imperial's flying boat services took quite a leisurely time to reach their Empire destinations. For example, Durban took five days with night stops at Athens, Wadi Halfa (Sudan), Kisumu (Kenya) and Mozambique (East Africa). And places like Singapore took five-and-a-half days. Singapore was as far as the Imperial crews went but the 'boats' went on to Sydney with Qantas (Australian) crews. There was also a flying boat service from Sydney to Auckland in New Zealand, so passengers could travel by flying boat right through from Southampton to Auckland.

Naturally, people nowadays like to think that before the Second World War things were rather primitive. But this is not really the case. The Empire boats had very comfortable seats with plenty of leg room. They flew at around 10,000 feet so the passengers had a good view of the country they were flying over. There were very few planes then and very few regulations, so there was nothing to prevent the airliners from coming down low to see such sights as the Corinth Canal or the Pyramids. And an absolute must then was the Bor herd of elephants. This was the biggest herd of elephants in the world and it was to be found in the Nile swamps of the Sudan. The flying boat skippers used to check up on its position and see that this was passed on to their colleagues. So it was quite usual for the 'boat' to come down to perhaps 50 feet above the swamp so that the passengers could see the great crowd of animals and perhaps photograph them. But they had to have a clear space to stand and big windows through which to see the view. And the Empire Boats had quite a large area with no seats at all but with big windows at shoulder height. This was rather suitably named the Promenade Deck and was very popular with the customers.

I can hear someone say, 'Well, of course the food and service were no good in those pioneering days!' Wrong! Imperial Airways had quite a different policy from today. The Steward was given a grant for buying the food for the voyage and it was made quite clear to him that tips were allowed. The Catering Manager made it rather obvious to him: 'If the passengers like the food and service they will give you a good tip at the end of the trip. So it's up to you to keep them happy.' And in those days the tips were certainly pretty big. Peers and judges were often carried out of England and gold and diamond millionaires ex South Africa. So the Steward often ended his trip quite a prosperous man. And did the rest of the crew benefit too? I am afraid not; you see those were the days when Officers did not expect tips! Though maybe one of the Captains might perhaps sometimes accept a gold Rolex from a millionaire. But the rest of the crew were certainly never offered anything.

So what sort of thing did we eat? Well, the meals had to be the sort of thing which could be carried in a Thermos flask. Naturally, scrambled eggs were usually served for breakfast and curry and rice was popular for lunch. And was the food really nice stuff? Certainly it was! It all came from the kitchens of the excellent hotels which Imperial Airways used. We have all got used to the packaged meals which are often served today on a tray. And we have rather forgotten the much more leisurely style of things before the War. In the late Thirties passengers had their lunch served on a table covered with a neat white cloth and the courses, starting perhaps with smoked salmon and ending with fruit salad and cream, were served in order and washed down with sherry, really good wine and port. And if passengers wanted some exotic cocktail? Well, the chances were that the very experienced Imperial Airways' Steward would know just how to mix it.

As I've told you, the air trips down the route were much lower and more interesting in the early days. This was not only because the Captains brought the planes down to see scenic attractions like the Abu Simbel Temple next to the Nile at Wadi Halfa, but also because the Captain or First Officer used to visit the passenger cabins quite often, carrying the map panels on which the route was marked. And we would show the passengers exactly where we were. In the evening there were often places of interest to see and a bus was laid on. For example, on the first evening of the trip passengers stayed at the splendid George the Fifth Hotel in Athens and the bus took them to see the Acropolis by moonlight.

People nowadays have some wrong ideas about the actual landings and take-offs on the flying boats. These were not at all the exciting splashy affairs the novelists sometimes put in their books. Almost always they were very smooth and gentle and sometimes the Steward had to wake passengers and tell them we had arrived. Just as a matter of interest, I personally flew flying boats for seven years and never had a difficult or dangerous take-off or landing.

Here are the details of my first exciting flight on these marvellous machines: the whole Imperial Airways' service to South Africa was not only very slick and efficient, but it was also extremely popular with passengers, who could either stay overnight at a New Forest hotel or come down in the special Pullman Express which travelled non-stop from Airways Terminal at Victoria. The train also brought the mail, freight and passengers' heavy baggage. All of this was put on board the waiting flying boat within minutes of the train reaching the quayside.

Imperial's marine staff brought the then extremely stream-lined and modern-looking aircraft over from Hythe and secured it tail-first in the flying boat dock, moored alongside the quay, at least an hour before scheduled departure. Once it was there we crew members and the engineering staff got on with our work. The First Officer had to do a careful inspection of the machine both inside and out, while the duty ground engineer ran up the engines and got them nice and warm for a quick take-off.

I went round the machine with the 'real' First Officer and then joined him when he inspected the weather forecast, made a flight plan and checked the early details of the load sheet.

Captain Rotheram arrived shortly before the train and the passengers arrived, and in a few minutes his practised eye was putting the finishing touches to the flight plan, checking the fuel load and making sure the aircraft was clean and ship-shape. Then, as the passengers trooped down the gangway and went on board, the skipper signed the loadsheet, the Steward made a final check that all his food and drink was on board, the hatches were closed and we were ready to go. I should perhaps add that the passengers did not have to get into a cold aircraft as the cabin was warmed up for them with portable heaters which the ground staff took off with them.

The start-up was simple. As the flying boat was held firmly in the dock, by a rope secured to a release hook on the back of the hull, the Captain could start all four engines and check switches before leaving. This done he ordered 'Release Tail'; the First Officer tugged the handle in the cockpit roof, and my first trip as a fully fledged crew member had begun.

The four Pegasus engines purred away with their characteristic singing noise and 'Ted' Rotheram ran inners and outers in turn to maximum power, and then began to ease all four gently open. In a matter of seconds the big boat had climbed on to the step and was planing along on top of the water with the bow wave going out behind us and the little waves slapping gently on the hull bottom. On each side, but at a safe distance, there were various surface vessels, small and large, and as the skipper pulled the machine into the air we passed the upwind launch flying its huge green flag, marking the end of the suggested take-off run. In practice, of course, we could have run for several times the 30 seconds of our take-off, because we were heading towards the Isle of Wight, many miles away.

The flight over France to Marseilles took four-and-a-quarter hours, during which time the Steward served an excellent hot breakfast, on the good, solid tables then provided. At the same time the Purser made sure that the mail bags and the baggage were neatly stowed in the right order of embarkation and he started on the ship's papers for the next leg from Marseilles to Rome. Once the aircraft was up at its usual cruising height of 8,000 ft with the autopilot engaged, the skipper went below (the cockpit and part of the mail stowage was on the top deck) to enjoy his breakfast and to chat to the passengers, who did not have to stay in their seats. They were allowed to walk around the promenade deck, which was especially popular with cine enthusiasts, who could 'take' the mountains of the Massif Central as we sped past them.

I suppose one of the reasons why all of us who flew 'boats' were so keen on them was the greatest contrast between the ugly uniformity of aerodromes and the beauty and variety of flying boat bases. Marseilles, our first landing on this, my first trip, was a charming place. We landed on the big lake, the Etang de Berre, set in pleasant open country outside the city. Everything worked with split-second precision. The skipper eased the big 'boat' gently down to the water; there was the murmur of a whooshing noise as she settled into the water; then we could feel the waves slapping enticingly against the hull; and with the skipper keeping power on and using the controls till the last minute to keep the wings level we came down off the step and became a quiet, slowish boat instead of an aeroplane.

Almost at once, with Gallic shouts and waves, the control launch dashed across our bows and threw a line to the Radio Officer waiting in the mooring compartment. In a moment our engines were switched off and the launch was towing us with typical French verve, and at great speed, towards the solid stone quayside. I must, I think, have blenched a bit, because the First Officer pointed out the huge arrangement of fenders stretched on ropes ahead. The French coxswain was a man of fine judgement, for a few seconds after he dropped the tow-line and shot out of our way we came to rest neatly and slowly against the fenders. One of the shore staff instantly tied our bows securely, whilst another lowered a specially designed gangway, and in a moment or so we were all able to walk ashore.

Refuelling was part of the First Officer's duties so, as soon as the flying boat was secure, we were taking lines from the fuel barge, which now came alongside. The Empire Boat was one of the first machines to have 'integral' refuelling, through a single fuel connection low on the starboard side of the hull. Getting the gas on board was, thus, so quick a process that 35 minutes after arriving at Marseilles we were off again. After another quick, short take-off, Captain Rotheram put the big four-engined machine into a fairly steep turn, which was perfectly safe with the low wing loadings of those days, and soon we were crossing the French Mediterranean coast and heading for Rome.

On this next leg of our journey I had a chance to check on the performance of the C Class, in service and with a full load. I found that after a fairly brisk climb, averaging around 500 feet per minute, the well-streamlined, all-metal machine cruised along at between 145 and 150 mph and used 105 to 120 gallons of fuel an hour.

The flight to Rome took 2 hours and 40 minutes and on the way we had a good view of the beautiful islands of Corsica and Elba, though many of the passengers were now having a sleep, encouraged by the good leg-room and fully adjustable chairs. It is perhaps worth recording that the C Class had head rests which could be adjusted up and down according to the passenger's height, a feature not found in many of today's jets.

The alighting area for Rome was on the sparkling Lake Bracciano, set in low green hills just north of the city. Here I was disappointed to find that passengers had to disembark on to a launch, as there was no flying boat dock. But even so the whole operation was so well organised that we were able to send the passengers ashore for a coffee, put the fuel on and get going again all in 35 minutes.

Our next call was at the old Roman port of Brindisi across on Italy's Adriatic coast. The flight was over land, of course, and the weather being 'gin' clear Ted Rotheram took the low level route through the mountain passes of the Benevento Gap. This again gave the keen photographers among the passengers some good mountain views. And in only 2 hours and 10 minutes we reached Brindisi, unfortunately an ugly little town where passengers did not go ashore for more than a few minutes. Refuelling was completed and we were on our way to Athens in only 25 minutes.

The final flight of a longish day was the 2 hours and 25 minutes across Greece to Athens. This, as evening began to approach, was a really beautiful flight. Our track took us first of all past Corfu, in my view the most attractive of the Greek

Islands. Then we headed up the long narrow Gulf of Corinth with the mountains rising on both sides. And finally, just as the sun set, Captain Rotheram brought us in to a silk-smooth landing on the unruffled waters of the Bay of Athens.

We are all so accustomed now to the idea that, whether the passengers like it or not, airliners simply fly on and on, 24 hours of the day, without taking any account of the need to sleep, that it is worth emphasising that, in 1938, even a long-distance flight, like that from Britain to South Africa, stopped every night. And arrangements were usually made for excursions. So having reached Athens we all, passengers and crew alike, went to the Hotel Grand Bretagne in the centre of Athens for a night-stop, if admittedly rather a short one. And a guide was already there offering a trip to the Parthenon. Like most of the passengers I decided that just for this one night I would sacrifice a bit of sleep and see the Parthenon by moonlight. I was, after all, only supernumary crew and I judged that when on the next trip I had all the First Officer's jobs to do I should want to get all the sleep there was going. It was certainly a worthwhile experience.

The rest of the trip went on in the same way. We were up for a dawn take-off from Athens and sailed serenely across the Med to land in the harbour at Alexandria in Egypt, where Imperial Airways had an engineering base. After an hour there we sped across the Nile Delta to land at Rod el Farag almost in the middle of Cairo. Quite an experience this, with only a small space of cleared water, outside which the huge Nile sailing craft were beating up river against the powerful current. Once again I was amazed at the speed with which first the passenger launch and then the fuel barge came alongside. But the other First Officer told me that the coxswains of each craft had to make an official report if they took longer than three minutes after the flying boat had moored up before they were alongside it. So no wonder we were off again in just 27 minutes.

In those happy days there was the minimum of ground interference with what an aircraft Captain might wish to do. So, in common with most Imperial skippers, Ted Rotheram

38

made a slight detour on the flight down to Wadi Halfa in the Sudan so that the passengers could see the Pyramids. And great was the clicking and whirring of cameras as we sped past at low level.

The longer flight down to Wadi Halfa took three-and-threequarter hours and was quite a lesson in geography and economics. A low level flight down the Nile shows Egypt's problems only too clearly. The vast mass of the country is stark, barren desert, and only a few oases and the narrow strip of fertile land along the great river provide an area where people can live. In consequence, the intensely green Nile Valley teems with people in town after town and village after village.

As the big boat sailed on over green valley or yellow desert, over raging cataracts and great placid stretches of water, dotted with the white sails of the feluccas (Egyptian native boats), I noticed that no attempt whatever was made to follow the course of the river. As Ted Rotheram said to an enquiring passenger: 'You are much better off in a flying boat, with its strong hull, than in a landplane with its thin fuselage, if – which God forbid – you should have to make a forced landing on land or water.'

At last there was the little town of Wadi Halfa ahead of us and soon we were sliding almost imperceptibly on to the smooth, tranquil waters of the Nile. Later, as we sat on the cool terrace of the Nile Hotel, perched on a bluff overlooking the river, we could see the flying boat moored to its big red buoy, as the brown river rushed by. The grass and trees on the river bank completed the peaceful scene. 'What a contrast,' I thought, 'to the dust, concrete and the heat of a land airport.'

The next day brought another early start but no one was at all tired, because we had been ashore from 3 o'clock one afternoon to 4.30 the next morning. There was, of course, a very good reason for the early departures in that period of civil flying. Lack of oxygen meant that the maximum height one could fly was around 10,000 feet, quite a smooth level in the morning but one that became increasingly bumpy as the sun took its effect in the afternoon.

Our first landing after just three hours was at Khartoum, and as we came into land and the passengers were able to get a good view of the twin cities of Khartoum and Omdurman, as well as the two great rivers, the White and Blue Niles, which join here. The difference in colour can be seen very clearly from the air, though to be honest, the Blue Nile seemed black, while the White Nile seemed yellow.

The flight from Khartoum to Malakal, another three-hour leg, interested me because of the sudden change in the character of the country, from yellow desert, with some dull greenish cotton areas, in the north, we suddenly found ourselves flying over the greenest of green lands with many high trees, and Malakal, when we reached it, seemed obviously an African, rather than an Arab, town.

A quick refuel here and we set off for Butiaba, a sleepy little settlement in Uganda, on the Albert Nile, so called because it flows out of Lake Albert. This three-hour and 40-minute section of the route did not at the outset look very promising. As on the other sections, I spent my time writing up the large, complicated instrument log, trying my hand at navigation, and with Ted Rotheram's permission, taking the automatic pilot out and flying the machine myself. But around the middle of the flight the skipper and the other First Officer and the Radio Officer all concentrated on one thing, spotting the great Bor herd of elephants. This spectacular sight, 150 or so huge beasts of all ages, was almost always to be found in the fertile pastures and forests near the little town of Bor. Suddenly the Radio Officer shouted, 'There they are, Sir,' and in a second Ted Rotheram had taken out the automatic pilot, put the aircraft in to a turn, and blown his whistle to summon the cabin crew. As we swept down towards the huge black patch in the sea of green the Purser appeared. 'There you are, Purser,' said the skipper, 'the Bor herd – right on the nose. Tell the passengers I'll be doing a complete circuit of them – keeping them on our left all the way.'

What a sight it was – in fact for the passengers I should think it was the sight of a lifetime. As the huge 'boat' circled round the herd at about 50 feet from the open grassland, the bulls advanced, trunks waving and huge ears flapping. In the background the cows and the young elephants retreated towards some nearby trees. This little diversion from straight and level flying took maybe five minutes, but what dividends it paid in terms of satisfied passengers.

Incidentally, one of the things which impressed me about our whole Imperial Airways service was the great attention paid to the passengers. Apart from highlights like the Bor herd, every effort was made to keep them happy. When he could spare the time, and at least once in every long leg, the Captain would take a map down to the passenger cabins and show all the passengers where we were. In between these visits, position reports were made out by the pilots and taken round the cabin by the Pursers, who also circulated the news bulletins, which the Radio Officers were able to get from time to time.

The next flight over Uganda, from Butiaba to Port Bell on Lake Victoria, was very attractive. After thousands of miles of deserts and jungle it was pleasant to see farmlands, tea and coffee estates and neat-looking little villages. But there was also another sensational sight, the Murchison Falls, on the Victoria Nile. The whole flood of the river plunges down through a small gap in the wooded hills sending clouds of spray into the air. And as the flying boat flew past at tree-top level, the passengers had a grand view, not only of the falls but of the hundreds of crocodile and hippo, disporting themselves in the pool below.

Port Bell, with its neat, well-painted landing stage and passenger buildings, seemed a typical little bit of the Empire, which then certainly seemed a fine achievement to me. It was a pretty place with gently rounded green hills on each side of the long narrow lake harbour.

The final leg of an exciting day took us across the huge and beautiful Lake Victoria to Kisumu in Kenya, then one of the Empire's proudest possessions, and a place where European settlers confidently expected to remain for generations. We flew at about 4,000 feet above sea level but only a few hundred feet above Africa's biggest lake. It was all very idyllic, with one or two yachts, some native fishing boats, one old lake steamer, with passengers waving from the deck, and lots of lush, round, green islands. And then there was the town and port of Kisumu, shining in the evening sun, on one side the red earth of the runways at the land aerodrome, then the slipway, buildings and mooring buoys of the flying boat base and then the red and green painted roofs of the town. And with the usual quick half circuit of the alighting area, Ted Rotheram swept in to land on the mirror smooth waters of the lake.

I enjoyed the evening in the old Kisumu Hotel, one of the real old colonial establishments, with excellent local food, good service, and a good sleep under my mosquito net in a cool airy bedroom. A stroll in the evening took me down to the Kisumu Club, where the other First Officer and I sampled the local beer, not bad stuff called, appropriately, 'Tusker', and brewed in Nairobi.

At Kisumu, Ted Rotheram and his crew handed over the service to Captain 'Carlos' Madge, an Anglo-Chilean, and there was a change of aircraft too, with our 'boat' being towed on its beaching chassis to the hangar for some routine maintenance.

Our next day took us via the big Kenya port of Mombasa, the equally large Tanganyika port of Dar-es-Salaam and the little town of Lindi to our night-stop at Mozambique, then in Portuguese territory. My remembrance of the trip concerned largely the food. There was the best breakfast of the trip with excellent Kenyan eggs and ham; and one of the best lunches with Kenyan crayfish salad, followed by really luscious local mangoes.

Although the flying boat base at Mombasa was quite charming with a huge stretch of sheltered water, Dar-es-Salaam must rate as one of the prettiest harbours in the world. It was almost circular and nearly land-locked, with a sandy beach along the shore and several fine old German Colonial buildings lining the harbour.

Lindi was not particularly interesting but Mozambique, when it came into view, was a splendid little town. There were some fine old Portuguese houses and churches and it was one of the oldest towns in Africa, having been established by Portugal in the sixteenth century. But it did not boast a good modern hotel and this in 1938 gave Imperial Airways the excuse for providing the most unusual passenger accommodation on their routes. They bought the old Durban Harbour tug, the *Dick King*, and converted it into an excellent houseboat.

The *Dick King* provided pleasant little cabins for passengers and crew, refreshing showers, cool, breezy deck space for enjoying a sundowner, and quite a fine dining saloon. But best of all after a long day's flying there was a large fixed gangway from which you could enjoy a swim in the clearest, cleanest water imaginable.

I now had only one day's flying ahead of me before I would be seeing South Africa – my wife-to-be's homeland. Naturally I was all agog, having heard a lot about it.

Inevitably I did not take a lot of interest in the long stretches of flat country, interspersed with the mouths of great rivers which made up Mozambique, then rather an undeveloped country. Though the mouth of the Zambesi was so gigantic that one could scarcely fail to notice it; like the Sudan it was a great haunt for elephants and once during the flight Carlos Madge brought the 'boat' sweeping down close to the ground so that the passengers could see an enormous herd of buffalo, on one side of the plane, and a smaller herd of elephant on the other.

At last after a total of nine hours, mostly flying over the rather featureless countryside of Portuguese territory, there ahead of us was a great city. Durban was wonderfully situated. Behind the city was the Berea, a great wooded hill, spotted all over with fine homes. Then there was the sea front, a fine promenade area with huge hotels, blocks of flats, a golf course or two, and the race course. Further south lay the great land-locked harbour, in those days lined with merchant ships of every size and nationality, tied up to the great expanse of quays. While the city side of the harbour was fully built up and developed, the seaward side was, in 1938, still quite wild. It consisted mostly of a long, wooded hill called the Bluff, and had only a small hotel and a few holiday bungalows on it.

And there, at the end of the harbour, was the usual control launch flying its huge green flag to tell Captain Madge that the area was clear for his landing. So, forty-eight-and-a-half hours' flying and five days after I left England on my first ever trip with Imperial Airways I reached Durban in South Africa. Some may say that it took an awful long time. That may be so, but I can assure you that I have seldom seen so many happy and grateful passengers as those who stepped ashore in Durban that day more than 60 years ago.

3

War, Marriage and a Move

My first trip to South Africa was followed closely by another trip on which I was at last pulling my weight as a fully-fledged First Officer. And quite an exacting, hard-working job I found it to be. The hours would certainly now be thought to be pretty long. Ten hours flying a day, with at least thirteen hours on duty, could be quite tiring, especially as it was likely to be succeeded by only around five hours' sleep. But there was certainly time off down the route. This second trip of mine was to Kisumu and back and I had three rather enjoyable days off there, with some golf and some walking beside the lake in the pleasant Kenya climate. But that was all. Of course, on the longer trip to Durban there was a stand-off both ways in Kisumu as well as three days in Durban, which was not bad. On the other hand, the total trip was seventeen days away. Finally the stand-off time in England between trips would certainly not have pleased the Pilots' Association of today. Even after the longest trip, the twenty-day voyage to Singapore and back, we only got a week back at base.

I didn't resent this at all. I thought the Empire Boats were marvellous aircraft; Imperial Airways a great company; and flying the best life ever. Mind you, we were in many ways extremely well treated. Amazingly, the Company insisted on the same absolutely top-grade hotel accommodation for the crew as they gave the passengers. And in the matter of transport we fared even better, with a big saloon car to take us to and from the night-stop hotel, while the passengers took a bus!

The trips we did to Singapore were part of the other great Empire Route, that connecting Southampton with Sydney and later with Auckland, New Zealand. We only ever got as far as Singapore, worse luck. So it was years before I saw that great country New Zealand. But the trip to Singapore certainly gave me an excellent picture of a huge slice of the British Empire.

A few pictures stick in my mind about the long haul through Palestine, Iraq, The Gulf, India, Burma, Malaya and Singapore. Palestine always conjures up memories of the clear cool waters of Lake Tiberias on a hot summer's evening. It was our pleasant custom to send the passengers with the Purser, whose job it was to look after them at night-stop stations, up to the hotel, and then to swim ashore ourselves from the flying boat. Excellent exercise which made tea on the hotel terrace later doubly welcome.

Iraq was never one of my favourite countries, but at least when it was under British influence it seemed to be making excellent progress, and was entirely peaceful and law-abiding. Basra was, in fact, one of our most up-to-date night-stop stations, with a permanent electric flare-path in the Shatt-al-Arab river, boat moorings and the landing stage right in the hotel grounds, and, wonder of wonders for those days – there was an excellent air conditioner in the bar!

Bahrain's only good feature for me was that there was a decent swimming club and Imperial Airways would arrange for us to spend the day there if we were ever delayed.

Dubai, on the other hand, I thought charming. Much cooler than Bahrain, it had a very attractive alighting area – a creek with almost impossibly clear, blue water bordered by old Arab houses, little mosques and lines of graceful dhows, belonging to the Sheikh's smuggling fleet. And, if you ever did have to spend the night there, you were taken to neighbouring Sharjah, where Imperial Airways had civil aviation's only real live fort complete with armed guards and battlements.

India under the Raj had, of course, many drawbacks. There

46

were great inequalities of wealth; there was a lot of snobbery; and low-caste Indians were certainly not allowed much dignity or self-respect. Nevertheless, Karachi was to us young pilots a very satisfactory slip-station, as we called a place where we had a day or so off-duty. We used a nice old hotel kept by an Englishman, where you could rely on wholesome food and absolutely clean bedrooms and bathrooms. We were members, automatically, of the Sind Club, with its squash court and fine old cool lounges and dining room, and the Gym Club with its dances, billiards and tennis courts. Then if we wanted to get away from it all we could hire a bunder-boat (a sort of sailing water-taxi) and go off for the day with cold beer and a picnic lunch to a nearby beach called the Sandspit. Another memory is of being approached by a very prosperous and well-spoken gentleman, who tried to persuade me of the huge profits to be made by smuggling precious stones into Britain. I can't say I was much tempted.

Calcutta, mercifully never more than a night-stop station, was certainly an experience. The incredible mass of surface craft all over the alighting area on the great River Hooghly, with the Indian Police whacking their crews with lathis (Indian truncheons) if they did not make way for the flying boat quickly enough; the wild, mad driving of the Sikh taxi-drivers; and the awful contrast between the poverty in the streets and the Indian nobility in the Great Eastern Hotel, positively dripping with jewels; these impressions will never leave me.

Further east from Calcutta and life got better and better. Rangoon in Burma, then known as the Scottish Colony, was a very clean, dignified and prosperous place with a huge export trade in timber, oil and rice. What a pity that it has now become such a troubled, poverty-stricken country. I did not see much of it in the days of the Raj but the general air was always of constant, efficient activity.

Bangkok in those days was the kind of fairy-tale city you really enjoyed visiting. The river running through the city, on which we also, incidentally, landed, was not only apparently pretty clean, but it also was a mass of graceful looking canoe-type boats. These, as often as not, were paddled by beautiful

Siamese girls, who sensibly judged that they would be more comfortable stripped to the waist. Restaurants, hotels and cinemas were all clean and modern and the Siamese people seemed not only happy but also very friendly too.

Imperial Airways used the Oriental Hotel, a splendid establishment with a lawn right down to the river bank and I recall rather an amusing incident there. Normally, most of the passengers were either men or ladies travelling with their husbands. But as luck would have it on one trip we not only had a plane-load of women passengers but the hotel was also extremely full. Mrs Robins, the proprietor of the Oriental, had to ask the ladies to double up, a most unpopular move. First of all she asked them to arrange it among themselves, but they were not at all helpful.

'Well, ladies,' she said, 'we cannot stand here all the evening. I must allocate the rooms myself.' And she read out the names in pairs. All hell was let loose.

'I'm not sharing with that woman.'

'Well, thanks, dear, and if you think I want to be in the same room with you ...' And so on, *ad infinitum.*

The patient voice of Mrs Robins cut through the hubbub.

'Ladies, please. I have another suggestion. Behind you you see the gentlemen of the crew. They are, I am sure, very gallant. Now, which lady would like to share with the Captain? And who will share with the First Officer?'

We beamed with pride and anticipation, but alas, with enormous speed, the good ladies chose partners from their own sex and vanished, blushing, to their rooms.

But perhaps the best place of the lot on the Eastern Route was our destination, Singapore. Everything was good about it. The traffic and engineering people were remarkably quick and accurate in all their work. And they were the champions in the genial rivalry between the various stations on who could attach the beaching legs to a flying boat fastest and tow it up the slipway.

The hotel used by Imperial Airways was the magnificent Sea View. It had everything: an enclosure for safe sea bathing; a huge, semi-open-air dining room with space for dancing (a band played three times a week); and right at the back of the hotel was a decent little nine-hole golf course. The Company bedrooms were excellent. Both Captain and First Officer had a big bedroom with private bath and we shared a roomy, airy sitting room.

Just down the road was the Singapore Swimming Club, a very impressive place where all sorts of parties took place, as well as water sports.

This, then, was my life in those happy years just before the Second World War; alternative trips included Durban, Singapore, Kisumu and the short trip to Alexandria. As a co-pilot I wrote up the instrument log, did most of the navigation, refuelled the machine and on many stations did minor repairs, such as plug, magneto or even cylinder changes. There was also opportunity for flying practice. The skippers needed the experience themselves to begin with but later on we began to get three or four landings or take-offs per trip.

When I was able to get a trip out to Durban, my fiancée Joanie came down to see me and on one occasion we made our engagement official by getting a nice little diamond ring at Randle Brothers and Hudson in Durban. Arrangements were made for us to get married in the autumn of 1939 and we had plans for a proper honeymoon in South Africa.

There had been another development around this time. Imperial Airways had unwisely sacked some pilots for joining BALPA, the pilots' Union, and had therefore attracted quite a lot of adverse publicity. The whole affair ground on for many months with a Government enquiry into the state of British Civil Aviation. As a result the private enterprise Company ceased to exist and a new public Corporation, British Overseas Airways, was set up by merging Imperial Airways with British Airways. Although we were all pleased to have a new management which would be compelled to recognise the Union, of which I was incidentally a founder member, we thought a lot of the other criticism of Imperial was unfounded. It seemed to me at the time that Imperial should have been given much more credit for their courage and initiative in buying the huge fleet of Empire Flying Boats and providing the first really practical, reliable through services to South Africa and Australia. However, with their customary ingratitude, the Government of the day pushed out most of the Imperial top brass and promoted a lot of British Airways people.

I have not mentioned British Airways much so far, because frankly it was a piddling little outfit with no important routes and it unpatriotically operated American machines at a time when our own designers and constructors were certainly in no way inferior to Lockheed, Douglas or Boeing.

I am dwelling a bit on this shabby treatment of Imperial Airways because it developed during the war and after it into an anti-flying boat and anti-British aircraft attitude which has done our country a great deal of harm. More of this at the right time.

All of us involved can recall the sense of an impending storm during the summer of 1939, so I will not go on about it much. As the summer came, I think everyone understood not only that war was coming but that Britain was far from ready for it.

Joanie and I were wondering how our plans were going to work out in this uncertain world. In effect, of course, by the time we were married on 28th October 1939, Britain and South Africa had already entered the war. This naturally put paid to the much jollier plans we had had for a big wedding in Johannesburg. With South Africa, like Britain, putting itself on a war footing, no one much was taking holidays. So it was a pretty quiet honeymoon as well as being a pretty quiet wedding.

The British authorities were aware of the strength of the Luftwaffe so they did not want to make it easy for that large force to start bombing our cities. As a result all the radio aids for airliners were cut off. And this in turn meant that Joanie and I were very nearly killed on our way home to England from our honeymoon in South Africa. The weather, as luck would have it, was atrocious and the Captain, our best man, Roger Mollard, could only feel his way towards England at low level below the clouds. One day we flew over the flattish south-western part of France from Marseilles to Bordeaux, and

50

then on to St Nazaire. The next day we attempted to fly across the Channel from St Nazaire to Southampton only to be forced back by low cloud. The third day we set off again, flying steadily lower and lower over the sea, until suddenly right ahead of us and very close the skipper and I saw the white cliffs of the Isle of Wight. By common consent we both gripped the control wheel and heaved it hard back; the flying boat surged upwards and we missed the cliff-top literally by inches. We still had to judge how long to stay in the cloud, before descending as we hoped over Southampton Water. And that was a nerve-racking business too, but finally we were back in England in one piece; and Joanie and I could say goodbye to the flying boat and to our best man, at any rate for a brief spell.

When war broke out many of us who were on the RAF Reserve, or thought we were, made investigations to see what our position was. The answer from the Air Ministry was that we were not now considered to be reservists, and it had been decided that, having been trained as commercial flying boat pilots, the best job we could do for the country would be to continue our present work. So that is what we did.

There were times during the war when I felt rather guilty about my relatively safe job. I shall always feel that the real heroes were Britain's bomber crews. Their courage and endurance in slogging across to Germany, despite flack and fighters, and getting their bombs to the target night after night, is something to marvel at. The fighter boys were great too but they had the excitement of the chase to buoy them up and the knowledge that much of their time they had better machines than the enemy. Looking back on it all I think we people in BOAC did as good a job as the ground personnel in the RAF or those engaged in non-combatant work like flight training. But we were no heroes.

The war made inevitable changes. Very rapidly we became more of a transport service for the RAF, Army and Navy than anything else. Almost all the passengers were fairly senior officers plus RAF pilots of all ranks. The only civilians were diplomats or the odd chap in Intelligence.

Gradually the number of seats on the machines was pushed up and naturally this necessitated both higher take-off weights and more power from the engines. But there was plenty of 'stretch' in the old boats and we had no trouble at the new weights and powers.

This was the time of the 'phoney war' and in Southampton, where Joanie and I lived, life carried on very much as though Britain had never declared war on Germany. Food was still plentiful and cheap. But my relatively pleasant life was suddenly shattered. Leaving my beautiful wife and my nice little flat one day in June 1940 I quite expected to be home again within the three weeks then taken for a voyage to Singapore. But when we reached Marseilles we were warned that French Intelligence expected Italy to join the war on Germany's side at any moment. We were therefore given the use of the many French flying boat bases around in order to bypass Italy. The route was certainly an odd one:

Marseille to Ajaccio in Corsica; Corsica to Bizerte in Tunisia; Tunisia to Malta; Malta to Corfu.

We spent the night in a charming if rather crumbling old hotel in this lovely island and found every one agog with the news of Italy's entry into the war. Paddy Sheppard, the genial Irish skipper with whom I was flying at the time, discussed the prospects of getting home again. Quite wrongly, as it turned out, neither of us was at all worried, thinking it would be quite easy to use some route along the North African coast.

So on we flew along our usual route with everything working according to plan until we reached Karachi, where we were in any case expecting a few days off. There we were met by Ronnie Geldard, then Station Manager for our agents, Indian National Airways, who showed us the cable from BOAC Head Office which read:

'All Services cancelled until new plans have been made following Italy's entry into the war.'

So while the planners sat down with their maps and wondered how to make the best use of the BOAC flying boats and their crews, we just stayed around in Karachi. It was certainly a worrying time for me. It is bad enough to be parted from

52

your wife after such a short period of married life but there was, of course, no way of knowing how she would get on in England, which I expected to feel much more of the effects of war. And it was anyone's guess as to when and where we should see each other again.

After ten days of this enforced inactivity the new plans were cabled out to us as follows:

'All flying staff at present out on the Eastern and Southern Routes are advised that they are now based in Durban, South Africa, from which point they will in future operate what will be known as the Horse-Shoe Route, connecting South Africa and East Africa with Cairo, and Cairo with Iraq, India, Burma, Malaya and Singapore. Staff are advised that their affairs in England will be wound up and their wives and families will be sent by sea to South Africa when shipping space is available.'

This was quite a staggering blow to us all and I, for one, certainly wondered how it would all work out. Naturally, I wanted to get down to Durban as soon as I could so that I could get on with finding a home for Joanie and for the baby we were expecting fairly soon. But when the services restarted some crews had to fly on out to Singapore before they could turn round and head for their new home in Durban. As it turned out I was one of the least lucky ones. Paddy Sheppard and I did, indeed, fly out of Karachi on 26th June 1940, but when we got to Singapore, we found there were many crews waiting there and it was not until 14th July that we finally pointed the bows of our flying boat in the right direction. But we had 11,000 miles through India and Egypt in front of us – 11,000 miles would even be a fairly long 'flog' these days but back in 1940 it seemed endless.

Not only did we have four or five sectors of flying each day but, as the Horse-Shoe Route was only operated once a week at the start, we had a week's stand-off at Karachi and a further week at Kisumu on the way to Durban. So it was not until 8th August 1940 that I sighted Durban as we flew down the Natal Coast from Lorenço Marques. And I certainly looked at the city with a great deal more than usual interest. It was, after all, likely to be my home for some time.

During all this time, although she could not let me know much about it, Joanie had been very busy. She was lucky to have her mother to help her as she awaited the Admiralty's pleasure in the matter of when a ship could be sent out to Durban. In fact she did not have as long to wait as she feared and was in Durban on board the *Windsor Castle* long before I got to South Africa. Naturally, the whole thing had been a tremendous strain and worry to her. So the baby she was expecting came rather before time. When I eventually arrived, I found I had a daughter, Jennifer Jane, as well as a wife waiting for me.

Luckily, we soon found somewhere to live. Considering there was a war on we were quite a fortunate young couple. As BOAC, like all British companies, held to the illusion that all foreign countries were more expensive to live in than Britain, we had a useful extra income, the £135 a year Durban allowance. This little sum enabled us to get a smart but very feeble Austin 8 Saloon.

4

Africa, Bournemouth and Africa Again

Life now settled down into quite a pleasant if sometimes rather an exhausting routine. Each voyage started at Durban, flew right through to Singapore via Cairo, and then returned the same way as far as Lorenço Marques, the colourful and slightly Latin capital of Portuguese East Africa. Then the flying boats flew inland to land on the great man-made lake, called Vaaldam, just opened as the flying boat terminal for Johannesburg, before finishing the voyage of 32 days at Durban. It would now be entirely illegal but we actually flew 175 hours in 32 days. Such a rate of flying was only accepted because, in the proverbial phrase, 'there was a war on'. And, at the insistence of the medical authorities, we pilots did a medical test every two months and we were supplied with a special 32-days' supply of vitamin pills in an effort to maintain our health.

Naturally, it was right that during a war we should have accepted this very heavy flying commitment. Others were, after all, risking their lives. But, as there is now so much discussion of the need to limit flying hours, it may be useful to record that when I was flying these very strenuous trips (they got even worse when Singapore was lost and the route became Durban / Cairo / Calcutta / Cairo / Lagos / Cairo / Durban or 200 hours in 32 days), I lost a stone in weight and contracted at one time or another malaria, jaundice and dysentery.

With this strenuous schedule BOAC found that they had to allow us at least three-and-a-half weeks in between voyages in order to maintain our health. Allowing for various duties in the office, plus standby duty, this still meant that Joanie and I had three weeks' holiday every two months. And very good use we made of it.

But the long voyages covering a big slice of the world continued. The Captains with whom I flew were now giving me more and more landings and take-offs and I was learning all the tricks of the flying boat trade. For example, at Beira and Mozambique we landed and took-off in big open stretches of water, often subject to heavy swells. If you do nothing about a swell then your flying boat will pitch up and down in a motion called porpoising and it can get quite out of control, so you have to damp the motion out by pushing the control column forward when the bows are coming up and pulling back when the bows are going down. This needs careful judgement, especially as at the same time you are probably using rudder, aileron and differential throttle to deal with a cross-wind.

Another problem you have with a flying boat is that of the glassy calm – the day when the surface of the water is like a mirror and you simply cannot tell when you are at the right height to pull the power off and make a landing. We developed a technique which worked just as well at night, or when the alighting area is blanketed out with fog, as it did with a glassy sea. This was to come down to about 200 feet on the altimeter, reduce the speed to about 95 mph and hold a rate of descent of about 200 feet per minute, with plenty of engine power. Then we just held the wings level and waited, keeping our eyes in the cockpit so we would not be tempted to judge a landing. As a system this worked perfectly and the worst that ever happened was that the boat would do a very slight bounce before settling into the water. The ability to land quite blind in fog gave the boat pilot a great feeling of confidence and was one reason perhaps why few boat pilots ever wanted to change over to landplanes.

All of us were now getting quite used to life around our long route. And really it was quite enjoyable. Cairo was one of the

56

places where we spent a lot of our days off. Here we lived in relatively cool comfort on a Nile steamer, moored conveniently next to the flying boat base at Rod-el-Farag. Even on the hottest day there was always a little breeze over the water and of course, as we were tied to a buoy out in the stream a bit, we avoided most of the mosquitoes.

Karachi was another spot where we were given time off. By this time we had a Mess in Karachi and were able to give ourselves quite decent rooms and not bad food in a town where the war was beginning to make both commodities rather scarce.

One of the things that I always found great fun was flying with an old skipper, called Daddy Foy. He was a perfectly good pilot but he had the habit of levelling the 'boat' out for cruising and then bursting into song. The words were always the same: 'I'll be a wild rover nay never no more. Nay never, never no more will I be a wild rover! Nay never no more!' What made it wildly funny was that he was the very opposite of a 'wild rover'! He was always impeccably dressed and well conducted in every way!

Late in 1941 it was judged that I had now learnt all about swells, glassy calms, downwind take-offs and blind landings and could therefore be promoted to the rank of Captain. This was, of course, a very proud moment in my life and I must own that I was very happy when, at 5.30 in the morning on 4th December 1941, I took off from Durban Harbour on my first trip in command. Suitably for a new Captain I was given a very experienced co-pilot, a chap I remember called 'Snakehips' Anderson, renowned for his athletic figure and his great success with the ladies.

Life, it seemed to me at this time, was pretty good. I had a wife and daughter I was very fond of. I was lucky to have a job which would go on after the war but still, I thought, was doing a reasonable job for my country, although of course others did more. I was flying a big efficient aircraft which was providing useful transportation for the war effort. We were moving senior officers, RAF pilots, important spares and so on from Africa, through the Middle East to India. And by providing a link across from the Nile to the Congo and then up to Lagos in West Africa we provided a through air service to England and America.

I should mention something about the route from Cairo to Lagos because it was not only an odd route for a flying boat but also rather important to the war effort. Facilities on the Congo were pretty rudimentary compared with those on the Nile. The weather was often very bad but there were few aids to navigation. Even the few radio beacons in use were not well sited for getting into our flying boat alighting areas, so we had to do a lot of contact flying. I remember one trip when, to get the service through, I had to follow the course of the Congo for many miles, keeping in the little gap between the water and the clouds which rested on the huge trees at the top of the high river banks. This so overcame my Purser that the Radio Officer, on going below, found him on his knees at his desk.

'What on earth are you doing, man?' asked the RO.

'I'm asking the Lord to save us,' came the reply.

'Get on with your work and trust the skipper,' retorted the RO before coming up to tell me of the Purser's fears.

In reality there was not really any risk in this kind of low flying because we had excellent charts of the river and the only obstacles we were likely to meet were the very few Congo steamers still operating. We used to land at Stanleyville and at Leopoldville, both in those days very clean, modern-looking Belgian towns.

At Lagos we pilots had a Mess which was really too comfortable for those war-time days and the standard of meals contrasted ill with the meagre rations in England. In particular the Palm Oil Chop, a splendid local chicken and rice dish served every Sunday for lunch, was a veritable feast!

I referred earlier to the resentment which we old Imperial Airways people felt about the advancement given to the staff from that tiny little outfit, British Airways. Even in 1942, the ex-BA people were already starting to talk about getting rid of flying boats, and concentrating on American landplanes. During my visits to Lagos I was able to dig out an extra-ordinary and revealing fact. This was that BOAC had the same number of flying boats as they did landplanes flying into Lagos, though the much bigger boats carried far more load than the landplanes, yet such was the greater reliability of the boats and their freedom from engineering complexity, that looking after them needed only half as many engineers as looking after the temperamental landplanes. One example will suffice of the truth of this argument. A landplane has to have a hydraulic system for its powerful brakes and its undercarriage retraction system. It also needs tyres, which of course wear out very quickly and an oleo-leg to absorb the shock of landing. All these items need frequent, expensive maintenance and part replacement. In comparison, the excellent Short Flying Boat needed no hydraulics, no brakes, no tyres and no oleo-legs. In fact the only maintenance on the equivalent of an undercarriage, the hull bottom, and the floats, consisted of occasionally drilling out a leaky rivet and, rarely, changing a plate in the hull bottom.

The war was not a time when anyone's life ran smoothly and in April 1942 several pilots from Durban were suddenly posted to a new BOAC base in Asmara, a big town and airport recently captured from the Italians in East Africa. Joan and I were very sad about this sudden posting but naturally, like everyone else, we put a brave face on it. The base was really necessary. With the increasing scale of the war operations in the Western Desert and other parts of the Middle East, the Service Chiefs demanded a greatly augmented air transport network centred on Cairo. They made American Hudson and Lodestar and British Flamingo aircraft available for the job, to join the big four-engined Ensigns which BOAC flew out from England. The base was at Asmara, because, as those more vitally concerned than myself will remember, Cairo was constantly under threat from the German and Italian forces.

The landplane training course which I now had to undergo was at Nanyuki in Kenya. So, although we were not at all sure that anyone but me would ever get to Asmara, the three of us set off for Kenya, where life turned out to be pretty comfortable. My course finished in May 1942 and I had to fly post-haste to Asmara. Poor Joanie could only get as far as Kampala in Uganda, then a very peaceful, prosperous and happy place. Asmara and air transport up to it was very much under Army control and my best hope was that in time I would persuade the military government to allow my wife and child to join me.

After a spell in the BOAC Mess I at last managed to get the promise of a flat and a long trip for Joan and Jen up the Nile on a steamer. And with this organised, the ladies of my family were allowed to join me. We all found life in Asmara a remarkable change from the old life we had known for 18 months in Durban. To begin with, Asmara, up in the mountains of Eritrea, was a very cool spot. The town lies at 7,600 feet and even if the days are warm the nights at that altitude are always cool. Then, even after their defeat by the British and South African forces, and the Indian Army, the Italians remained around Asmara in large numbers and the town was still unmistakably Italian in character. They ran all the shops, restaurants and hotels and were patriotically determined not to speak any English, even if they understood it. When Joan went shopping all her efforts were met with the reply; 'Non parla Inglese, solo Italiano'. So, on the principle that 'Si non parla Italiano, non mangare', we soon learned to talk away in pidgin Italian.

Our flat was No 14 Via Penazzi and if you accepted that it came with the compliments of the Billeting Officer it was not bad. It had a living room, dining room, two bedrooms, kitchen and bathroom, as well as a bit of a balcony. True, there were certain oddities, such as the scaldabagno, an incredible wood-burning geyser, and the rather ancient kerosine-burning cooker. Then the mains water was only turned on for a few hours every day, so you had to fill every receptacle in sight and remember to keep a bucket to flush the toilet. Joanie and I suddenly found interest in gardening and in the rather mad way of Britons who live at a very high altitude we simply made one out of the waste land behind our flat. The Italian woman in the bottom flat protested strongly, but I am sorry to say we took no notice. And we ignored also the Italians who used to come and watch us clearing away stones and rubbish and terracing our little garden.

'E non bono lavorare in Asmara,' they would say, 'troppo sole.' But we only answered, 'E bono per gli Inglesi'. Which goes to show that only the English 'go out in the midday sun'.

When the garden was finished we realised it was not much good without a wall around it. So off we went in a carrozza (an Italian horse-drawn cab) to the timber merchant. And here I have to report a strange lapse in my normally rather nonconformist standards of honesty. The merchant spoke English and was very frank.

'Signor Capitano, I have wood and I can make you a fence and two so beautiful gates. But of course it is vietato, completely forbidden. But, Capitano, at the airport there is a large dump of window shutters. I need 10 shutters for my house. You get me the shutters and I build your fence. Capito?'

Not only did I understand, but somewhat to my surprise I found and sweetened up an RAF corporal who undertook to produce a service lorry. In this we sailed happily past the guards, who saluted smartly, loaded the shutters, and drove out again, to another smart salute. The timber merchant was as good as his word and our fence and gates were much admired. Soon, to the astonishment of the Italian neighbours, we were growing Christmas trees and blue gums, white roses and some of the most enormous snapdragons I had ever seen. We watered the garden by flooding out all the bathwater on to it, as well as saving washing-up water and shaving water.

Although these happenings may indicate the contrary, in fact I had less time at home, compared with time away, than I had had in Durban. The system was simple. When an aircraft came out of the workshops it was allocated to a crew who took it up to Cairo. There they flew on all the various routes from Cairo to Adana in Turkey, Tehran in Persia, Addis Ababa in Ethiopia, Aden and Nairobi, until the time came for them to take a time-expired machine back to the engineers in Asmara. Then they got a few days at home and did the whole thing over again. The flying was very dull compared with the boats. To begin with it needed less skill to manage the small twin-engined machines we flew. Then the trips were shorter and did not go to very interesting places. During this period I had one of the few accidents of my flying life. We used to fly ex-RAF Hudsons with single controls, which was very hard on our co-pilots who got no flying practice at all. Foolishly, one day I took pity on my First Officer at Kano in Nigeria and changed seats to give him a landing. Even in those days Kano had an excellent runway, though it was across wind on the day in question. Although I warned the First Officer as we came in to keep the tail-wheel off the ground, he took no notice and did a typical RAF three-pointer. The Hudson, of course, behaved as they always do in such circumstances. It did a ground-loop and the undercarriage collapsed.

Hudsons had an evil reputation for catching fire so the crew and the 14 Polish Ferry Pilots were out of the machine and running in a matter of seconds and we all stood around waiting for it to burn. We were especially worried because we could see some fluid dripping down on to the runway. Just then an American Air Force car screamed up and out got the Station Top Sergeant (the equivalent of the RAF's Station Warrant Officer). In the way of such people he took charge at once.

'Now stand back all you guys,' he demanded, 'I'll just go and check this ship to see if she's a-going to burn.' And off he went, if rather gingerly. By this time there was quite a pool under the machine and very carefully he put his hand into it and raised it to his nose.

'Good God,' he exclaimed, 'beer'. And I remembered that we had filled the space under the seats with beer for the poor parched characters in El Geneina, where it was a pretty scarce commodity.

I have always been of the opinion that British aircraft are undervalued by our own people. So, although most pilots in Asmara used to try to avoid flying the De Havilland Flamingo, which they claimed was a death-trap, I used to take one from Engineering whenever they had one available. It was a very clever little machine – a high-wing monoplane with a big roomy cabin, a retractable undercarriage and two quiet, smooth, Perseus sleeve-valve engines. It was a much more attractive machine than the Lockheed Lodestars, which were its main competitors. Its take-off and landing runs were far shorter, its cockpit and cabin more comfortable, yet it cruised at 180–200 mph according to the power used, a very similar performance to the cramped little Lodestar.

The machine did have one serious disadvantage though, which incidentally caused the deaths of two friends of mine, Jock Barnett and Freddie Samuels. As with the Hudson, if you came into land rather slowly with the gear down on the continuous left-hand turn system, and then tried to straighten the aircraft out at the last moment, the wing just would not come up and you went spiralling into the ground. I developed the system of simply belting round the airfield with gear and flaps up at around 120 mph, then turning on to final approach at, say, 100 mph. With the field ahead I would bang the gear and flaps down and carry on in at about 85 mph. You could do this easily as the gear and flaps were worked by compressed air, from a huge cylinder in the cockpit, and went down in about five seconds. Anyway, using my method the Flamingo was as safe as a church and it is a pity that the top brass of BOAC never saw its merits.

This landplane flying was all go and we did not get very much time off either at the operations base in Cairo or the engineering base in Asmara. In Cairo we stayed at the Heliopolis House Hotel, where life at times had its exciting moments. The Luftwaffe used to come over from time to time with Stukas to bomb the overhaul hangars at Heliopolis Airport. The searchlights and guns were manned by the Egyptian Army and it was rather funny to notice that as soon as the first Stuka started its dive they would decamp, and firing and searchlight activity would only resume as the German machines headed for home. We used to sit happily on the balconies of the HHH, chatting with WAAF Officers who also used the hotel and drinking the coffee they brewed up, although in theory we should have gone to the shelters. It was really a vote of confidence in the efficiency and serious-mindedness of the German crews, who we rightly thought, would not waste bombs on an unimportant target like a hotel.

One evening the WAAF girls and ourselves were surprised to find the HHH invaded by a swarm of American Officers, all toting huge guns and wearing all sorts of medal ribbons. The girls naturally 'took the mickey' out of them a bit:

'Now tell me, sweetie, why are you wearing that great revolver, here, in Cairo?'

'Well, now, Ma'am, this here's a war-zone and old Uncle Sam's instructions are to wear hand-guns at all times in a war-zone.'

'But, my dear, the war is miles away, the other side of Alexandria. And after all, if a little woman like me isn't frightened, well why should a big man like you be?'

'And, Colonel, or whatever you are, do tell me about all those medals. Girls, come and listen. The Colonel is going to tell us how he won all those gongs.'

'Well, you know, honey, they ain't anything too special. This here's for leaving America and coming right across the Atlantic. This one here's for service in the British Theatre of War and this one here they just gave us for coming here to Africa.'

But the cream of the joke came later in the evening when the Luftwaffe arrived to do their always strictly accurate bombing of military targets. Great were the shouts from the corridor where the Americans were sleeping.

'Joe, Elmer, Harry, say, don't you guys hear the bombs going off?'

'We sure do, Charlie and we're on our way.'

'Right then, you guys, grab your hand-guns and get down to the shelter. Say, where's one of those Limies? Ah, there you are Mac, which way to the shelter?'

'But look, old chap, no one ever goes down there. The place smells too much of cat's piss. Anyway, why don't you just relax and join the girls here for a coffee?'

'Coffee, coffee, with these god-damn bombs falling all round the place. Come on boys, these Limies are just as plumb-crazy as we always heard they were.'

And with shouts, with great clumping feet, and with guns and cartridge belts flying, the American contingent went below, leaving the WAAF girls and ourselves curled up with laughter.

I suppose the most important job was to take Polish Ferry Pilots over to Lagos, where they picked up new American planes which had arrived by sea. This also had its amusing moments, this time because of American over-confidence. We knew from years of operation on the route that the maps in use were not accurate. And we had corrected our own maps. Wishing to be helpful we offered to allow the American-led formations to follow us, but with typical American independence they turned our suggestion down. As a result their formations were often overdue and sometimes even lost. The most amusing incident occurred at Malakal, about 300 miles south of Khartoum. A large American formation arrived there one day and the Colonel-in-Charge went to report to the Control Tower.

'Funny thing,' said the Colonel, 'I had no idea Khartoum looked like this. I expected it to be bare and sandy.'

'I've got news for you, Colonel,' said the British Airport Controller. 'You've just landed at Malakal and Khartoum is another 300 to the north!'

Meanwhile, our flying continued to all the places where we had troops. For example, we flew to Tehran in Persia where we were warned to have nothing to do with the Russians who were guarding the airport. Another destination was that horribly hot place Aden. I used to play squash there. The idea was that after you stopped playing and had a shower, you felt cool for just a little while! One of the advantages of the route was that we called in at Kamaran Island and exchanged Asmara vegetables for Kamaran fish. There were some big Ensign Airliners there and these were flown to Karachi and sometimes Delhi. They had been ordered at the same time as our Empire Boats but they were nothing like as successful. They had British Armstrong Siddeley engines and these were pretty unreliable and did not deliver enough power for such a big machine. By the way, it is interesting that the planes were fitted later with American Wright Cyclones and proved fairly satisfactory. But they always suffered from serious defects when compared with the Empire Boats. The first was that they did not have single point refuelling systems; you still had to pour fuel right into the top of the tanks and this took about twice as long as the quick 'boat' refuelling. Then the Ensigns used rather slow speeds on climb and descent. The upshot of all this was that, although the Ensigns cruised at 170 mph, against the boats' 155, the boats could do a leg like Basra to Karachi slightly quicker.

I suppose one of the encouraging things about the war years was that VIPs flew with us rather than with the RAF. We were just considered better! One of these kind of men I flew from Cairo to Lagos was the famous Admiral Vian. He travelled with his staff and was inclined to boss them about. So much so that another Admiral also flying with us said, 'For Christ's sake, Phillip, stop it!' The other Admiral was the senior man so Vian did in fact behave better! But he still had a go at me.

'Why do you fly these Flamingos at 190 mph? In the Navy we take them along at 200.'

'Well, Admiral,' I replied, 'I don't work for the Navy and my boss says keep the speed down to 190 mph.'

The British hold on Asmara was always rather shaky. In fact, when the Germans seized Tobruk, the Italians demonstrated in the main street, shouting 'Tobruk Tobruk' all down Viale Mussolini, as the High Street of Asmara was called. The only local garrison was a detachment of the Sudanese Camel Corps and a rather larger number of Sikhs from Jaipur. Our Garrison Commander decided on a show of strength and the troops marched along the main streets led by the Sikhs' Pipe Band. This seemed to quieten the Italians down a bit, but the most effective action came perhaps from Fitzyboy, as our Intelligence Officer was called. He took his small detachment of Red Caps and arrested the leading Italians and put them into the Cold Store. This certainly made them very quiet indeed. But it rather annoyed the Army Command and they sent General Selby down from Cairo! And he not only released the cold and miserable Italians but arrested Captain Fitzsimmons himself!

However, soon after this I stopped taking any interest in these Middle East matters. Malin Sorsbie, BOAC's Middle East Manager, was very polite about it.

'I'm awfully sorry about it, Howard,' he told me, 'but next Thursday you have to report to the RAF at Cairo West and they will fly you to Mildenhall.' Apparently the RAF had given BOAC 12 Sunderlands and Captain Jack Harrington had the job of finding people to fly them. They had been delivered to us without gun-turrets and with seats for 44 passengers and with civilian markings. So I and Captain Zippy Zorn were posted off to England. And what happened to our wives? Well, they were flown down to South Africa eventually but in the meantime we had to say goodbye to them. I heard later on that Joan and Jennifer were lucky enough to meet my friend Captain 'Biltong' Bellin in Khartoum and he gave them a lift to Durban. 'Biltong', by the way, was a South African and he got his nickname because he was fond of Biltong and always carried a stick or two of this South African dried meat in his briefcase.

First of all we flew to Cairo in a Lodestar; then we contacted the RAF transport people and were duly booked on a Liberator from Cairo West. We thought our machines were fairly 'hard-arse' but the RAF certainly carried people around in a still more primitive way. On the Lib we travelled in the bomb-bay, which was more or less sealed up for the purpose, but still perishing cold. The long flight to Gibraltar was cold enough, but the flight from there on to England in February 1943 was a real shaker. I had, after all, been in Africa since 1940 and my blood was pretty thin. Apart from the cold, the flight was very nearly the last I was to do. The Kiwi crew, though splendid chaps I am sure, were not too familiar with flying in the usual grim February weather. First of all they were unable to get into Lyneham and then decided to go to Feltwell, where it was hoped the weather would be a little better.

Of course, in the ordinary way going from Lyneham to Feltwell you would not go anywhere near London, but our Kiwi crew were, I think, flying contact and trying to map-read. For my part I was trying to see where we were too. First of all I thought there seemed a lot of suburban houses; then suddenly I saw a London bus. This was too much for me. I gripped the arm of an Air Commodore sitting next to me.

67

'Sir, do you see what I see?' I asked him.

'Christ-all-mighty, the bloody fools,' he shouted before charging up to the cockpit. A second later we turned steeply through 180 degrees as the Air Commodore came back to his seat.

'Those idiots were going to fly slap across London. Don't seem to have heard of the balloon barrage. We're lucky to be alive at all.'

Then, after carefully going out into Berkshire, down into Surrey, across into Kent and over the river to Essex, we made our way up into East Anglia. I was certainly relieved when we finally landed in ghastly weather. I still remember the Kiwis feeling their way around the fog-strewn field past rows of parked Sterlings, looking like so many giant statues in the mist, as they searched for the control tower.

We finally reached London by train around midnight, only to find that it was impossible to obtain any kind of a hotel room. Luckily for us at Airways Terminal, Victoria, the night-watchman took pity on us and gave us two of the emergency bedrooms they kept for the top brass who might have to stay in town.

The next day I went off down to Poole Harbour, where BOAC now had their Flying Boats Headquarters, known as Number Four Line. Jack Harrington was in charge, the same man who had first flown me in Imperial Airways before the war. He explained the situation to us:

'Look, chaps, the RAF have given us this fleet of Sunderlands and they want a daily service, through Foynes, Lisbon, Bathurst and Freetown down to Lagos. So I've called in all the boat pilots I can find. We're laying on a very brief refresher course on boats; giving you a very quick run around the Sunderland so you'll know its differences from the old C Class. Then it's going to be one run down to Lagos and back. And you'll be on your own.'

To my surprise Zippy Zorn objected. He wanted more training and a second trip with an experienced skipper down to Lagos and back.

'Now look here, Zippy,' said Jack Harrington, 'we're in the

middle of a war. I appreciate that there is a bit of a risk in this. And in peace-time I wouldn't do it. But I just have to get the show on the road. You can't have any more training and that's flat.'

'I just don't feel I can make it, Captain Harrington,' began Zippy again, but Jack Harrington cut in and spoke to me.

'Howard, for God's sake take Zippy out and get him to see sense. Surely he knows he just has to do as he's told for the duration.'

But I could do nothing with Zippy. In vain I assured him that the Sunderland was reputed to be easier and safer than the C boats. He would have none of it and I never saw him until years later when he was out of aviation altogether.

For myself, I just got on with the job. Raymond Winn, an excellent instructor, gave me about six hours' dual on the Sunderland, and I did my trip down the route with Reg Hallam, an ex-RAF man of about the same vintage as myself. I found the Sunderland a great improvement on the older boats. The longer nose made it easier to judge a landing and reduced the amount of porpoising on a swell. Then there were big improvements in the engines. Instead of the old two-pitch airscrews (equivalent to a two-gear motor car) we had proper constant-speed propellers, which could be set to give whatever pitch (the equivalent of gear ratio) was best for take-off, climb or cruise. This in turn meant we could get more power at lower engine revolutions, resulting in better speed, lower fuel consumption and longer range.

Naturally, there were no civilian frills. The only food was sandwiches plus coffee in Thermos flasks. We crammed seats in all over the big boats and got 39 passengers on board. The big fuel tanks enabled us to get up to ten hours' flying with a full load, quite a fantastic range for those days. Externally, the boats looked just like RAF machines, though the gun-turrets were removed and the roundels painted out. We had to be nominally civilian in order to land at neutral Foynes, the flying boat base on the Shannon in Ireland, and at Cabo Ruivo, the flying boat base on the Tagus near Lisbon.

Although there was some danger of being shot down by

German long-range fighters, it was on the whole an enjoyable assignment. We used to load up our nominally civilian customers, all dressed in sports coats and flannels, in the afternoon, and fly them over to Foynes. We waited until dusk before taking off again for Lisbon, where we hoped to land just around dawn. The idea was to avoid being found in daylight over the Bay of Biscay. If you were caught out in daylight, and saw any aircraft at all to the East, you immediately entered cloud, if there was any to be found. Otherwise there were two courses of action, both of which at times saved the lives of our crews. One was to dive down almost on to the water, knowing that a land-plane pilot is always too scared of water to get as low as you will. The other was to charge straight at the German aircraft and hope that he will take you for an armed Sunderland (an aircraft much feared by the Luftwaffe owing to its heavy fire power).

Once in Lisbon we again holed up for the day, to take off once more at dusk. From Lisbon we headed off into the night down the west coast of Africa. Port Etienne, our first point of call, was a miserable sandy hole, with nothing much there except the refuelling facilities and a radio beacon, and with the rather dodgy French attitude to the war we never got a very friendly reception. Luckily for us there had been a struggle here between the Vichy French faction and General De Gaulle and De Gaulle won. So BOAC had arranged for a Shell barge to be stationed down that part of the north-west African coast so that we could refuel there.

Bathurst, our next landing place, was a different kettle of fish. It had quite a cool, agreeable climate; there were proper BOAC staff and everything ran very smoothly. Unfortunately, we had to operate as fast a service as we could so we just had a quick refuel at Bathurst and pressed on to Freetown in Sierra Leone. Although this was quite a pleasant-looking town from the air and was set in fertile green country, it was very much not our favourite spot. We had a quick night's sleep there, our first night in bed since leaving England, but the RAF Mess which we used was extremely scruffy and uncomfortable. And the RAF chaps could not be expected to abandon cheerful parties just because a BOAC crew were trying to sleep. Mercifully, we only had one eight-hour leg the next day before reaching Lagos, and the very comfortable BOAC Mess. There we really slept the sleep of the just and we needed it. We had normally flown about 37 hours in four days, with just one night in bed, plus a rest in the afternoon in Lisbon.

Coming out from the austerities of war-time England it must be admitted that we enjoyed our two days off in Lagos. There were nice people to meet, masses of good food and quite a decent beach to go to. You could buy a big wicker basket full of eggs and a hand of bananas. And we used to take these highly prized things back with us to the Bournemouth Children's Hospital. We felt we needed to build up our strength for the flight back home, which was just as strenuous as the journey out. We simply left at dawn from the big, tree-girt Ikoyi Lagoon, and pressed straight on through Freetown to Bathurst, where we had a brief night stop. Off again next morning, we refuelled at Port Etienne and arrived at Lisbon at dawn. Then came another day stop in Lisbon and the flight home, via Foynes, with the Biscay leg of the flight done as far as possible in darkness. It was, to be frank, quite an exhausting job, but at least we felt we were doing something useful for the country.

Life at home in between the trips had its good and its bad moments. I shall never forget the day I arrived at Poole to be told that Ian Goalen, with whom I had had a beer the day before in Concha's Bar in Lisbon, had been shot down by the Luftwaffe. He and I had both left Lisbon at about the same time, though he was flying a Dakota, bound for Bristol, and I still wonder why they chose to shoot him down rather than me.

The German Airforce was very active around the British Isles and in the Bay of Biscay. I owe my life and the lives of some of my colleagues to the fact that not all Irish Station Commandants were neutral. One night in 1943 there were two of our Sunderlands and a Boeing Clipper waiting at Foynes for nightfall and take-off. And down the quay came the Irish Station Commandant. His words were: 'If I was one of you

71

boys I wouldn't be taking off.' We told him that we had to go or we would be accused of LMF (Lack of Moral Fibre).

'Oh well then, I'll have to spell it out to you! And hasn't the lighthouse keeper at Loop Head just rung me up to tell me that two German long-range Fighters are circling the mouth of the Shannon just waiting to shoot you boys down?' I told him that we were very grateful to him for not being completely neutral. He replied that he was not neutral at all and said: 'And haven't I just rung the RAF at Aldergrove and they said they'd just scramble three Hurricanes.' A few moments later our Irish friend was back.

'The lighthouse keeper says the Hurricanes have just arrived. And those bastards will never get home!'

While on the subject, my other 'close shaves' involved the very inexperienced navigators the RAF gave us. Luckily, I always did my own little bit of calculation, so when one night my navigator said, 'Captain, will you fly over Cape St Vincent Light over there?' I just said, 'No', because I had calculated that if we had indeed reached Cape St Vincent we would have been cruising at 174 knots and that is impossible in a Sunderland. The navigator was cross about it, but I was rather pleased when the RAF's Lisbon Intelligence Officer said, 'Well, Captain, I am pleased you're here! It means that you did not fly over the British Battleship Prince of Wales, which is just making her way down the African coast. Those bastards shoot you down first and find out who you are later.'

My other brush with 'the grim reaper' came on another night when my navigator suddenly said, 'Captain, will you turn ninety degrees to starboard?' Naturally I asked why.

'We've just reached the mouth of the River Tagus,' was the reply. Now, of course, if we were indeed where the navigator thought we were, we would have seen the bright lights of Lisbon. Instead it was all as dark as pitch!

'I'm going to circle where we are whilst you check things up on the local chart,' I told him. The navigator was wrong and we had several more miles to go to reach the Tagus. I ticked the navigator off but really he just did not have enough experience.

We had some excellent parties in Bournemouth, where we stayed at a clean, decent, private hotel, called the Cranborne Hall. Several nights a week there were dances at the large pub next door and we all enjoyed ourselves with the WAAFs and Wrens whose Messes were nearby. Such good evenings made one Sunday morning in Bournemouth even more tragic. The Germans swept in over the cliffs with canons blazing, lobbing off bombs in all directions. When it was over we found the WAAF Mess had been hit, right at lunch-time with most of the girls inside, and the pleasant little pianist with the band we had danced to was picked up dead in the park. Of course, there was the usual frantic search through the ruins of the various bombed buildings, but almost no one was found alive.

As I had become accustomed, just as I was settling down to the job at Poole, everything changed again. The BOAC bosses decided that the Sunderland was so much better than the old C Class that it ought to replace the Durban boats. So I was chosen to fly G-AGER, a very nice Sunderland with improved seating, out to Durban for Jimmy Alger, the manager out there, to have a look at. Naturally I was delighted to get this trip because Joanie and Jennifer were now happily installed at Torwood House, her father's nice old home in Forest Town, Johannesburg, and I might be posted back to Durban.

The trip out to South Africa was very pleasant and uneventful and I was pleased to show the machine off to Jimmy Alger, the Line Manager when I got down there. To my surprise he and the other bosses in South Africa were not at all impressed with G-AGER, and they decided almost at once that they would sooner carry on with the old C Boats. I did my best to point out to Jimmy Alger that the Sunderland would be able to cut out many of the stops on the old Horse-Shoe Route, and would thus speed up the services and cut down the costs. I have never understood why he turned the Sunderlands down and, in fact, I am sure he made a big mistake. If the Horse-Shoe could have been made really efficient, it could have been joined at Cairo with a service to the UK, for which the older boats were not suited. And if the Durban boats had carried on in peace-time, as well as the Poole boats, the anti-boat brigade would have had a harder job in getting rid of all marine aircraft. It's all in the past now, but I hope Jimmy will forgive my saying that I do not believe he appreciated the advantages of the low engine revolutions, low fuel consumption and consequent good speed and range characteristics, which the Sunderland, with its bigger, more modern power plants, possessed.

But, purely personally, the rejection of the Sunderlands helped my family life. I was now formally back in Durban and settled down to the old routine of the long trips around Egypt, India, the Congo and West Africa. And, of course, I was reunited with my wife and daughter and happily I arrived in South Africa for the expected birth of our son, John.

Flying the Horse-Shoe Route, with its two extensions to Lagos and Diego Suarez in Madagascar, was very much routine. The only problem was that we got rather tired, so when the Airline decided to try cutting down our three-and-a-half weeks between voyages to two-and-a-half weeks this was not at all successful. It seems a hell of a lot of flying nowadays but during the war it was not unusual to do voyages of 40 days. For example we flew from Durban to Calcutta, back to Cairo, across to Lagos, back to Cairo and down to Durban with a detour to Vaaldam, the marine airport for Johannesburg. When you consider that we only cruised at 155 mph, slept every night ashore and had to land to refuel every 350 miles or so, you can understand that it was quite hard flying. Anyway, we needed the three-and-a-half weeks to recover and when this was cut down to two-and-a-half weeks the crews started to go sick with things like influenza and sore throats. However, luckily the Airline soon learned that it was better to give their crews the time to get fit again, though we weren't ever really fit. For example, I had to take pills to suppress dysentery and malaria and we all took vitamin pills because during the war the food was fairly bad. All the Line Manager kept saying was that everything would be fine once the war was over.

BOAC were now getting set to expand when peace came and we started a big programme of training First Officers for command. Although I was not very senior as a Captain I was always considered fairly efficient on flying boats and I had the privilege, with South African 'Biltong' Bellin, of doing the final check-out trips before First Officers were promoted to Captain. And interesting work it was too, because in those days we made quite a distinction between just being a good pilot and being a good Captain. And I believe that the fact that many airlines do not stress this distinction so much today does have a bearing on the slight falling off in service to passengers you see these days and it could even be the indirect cause of one or two crashes. In the old flying boat days we were not only looking for men who could handle a boat well in any conditions of sea or weather, but also men with a bit of personality, with an obvious desire to give the passengers a good trip, and men with some knowledge of the company they were working for.

For instance, when I was sitting in the right-hand seat and assessing someone for command I would not give very high marks to a man who allowed the crew or junior ground staff to get away with undue familiarity, to someone who sat in the cockpit reading a book when there was some useful information he could be giving to the passengers, or to someone who invariably just followed the regulations instead of using his initiative now and again. This, frankly, was one of the great differences between the way the boats were run and the much lower standards that were accepted on landplanes.

It is perhaps worth recalling that some men who were, I am sure, quite good landplane pilots could not quite prove themselves really safe and capable at the most difficult 'boat' stations. An example is Luxor, which was used sometimes if a north wind made it doubtful whether the plane could fly the Wadi Halfa to Cairo leg. Luxor was nearly always rough with a cross wind and some pilots could not operate there. But the most difficult landing area on our routes was Jiwani in Baluchistan. This was not only short and across the prevailing wind but there was always a swell there. Now and again I had to take over from a landplane pilot who simply could not cope. He had to go back to Dakotas and stick to runways that stayed still!

Which is not to say I never had any close shaves myself. I was once caught out over Beira in Mozambique. The sad situation was that the piece of water we used there, the mouth of the Punguwe River was completely fogged in, and the alternatives at Inhabane and Quelimane were shut down through fog as well. So for the first time in my life I had to do a completely blind landing in a flying boat. Can a 'boat' do that sort of thing? Certainly it can and we used to practise the technique when we landed at the big Madho Sagor Lake at Gwalior in India. So when we only had 20 minutes' fuel left I carried out the Gwalior system for real! First of all I positioned myself over the BE Beacon; then I established myself on course for the alighting area; then I adjusted my speed to the 95 mph we needed; and finally I set the plane on a descent rate of 200 feet per minute. At Gwalior we were only doing it for practice with the Captain's seat set so low that he could not see the water. But now I was doing it because I had to. And it worked. Although I could not see a thing, the old 'boat' just splashed on to the water. It is rather splendid to think that at that time you could not possibly do the same thing in a land-plane. There was no Instrument Landing System and the aerodromes were too small anyway.

Here they let me make an honourable exception of the Atlantic landplanes where good standards were kept up. There was, of course, a big school of thought among the ground administration in BOAC, especially those from British Airways, that wanted 'biddable bus-driver' kind of Captains. In fact, I recall one of these people (whose name now escapes me) who said in my hearing: 'We've got to get rid of the flying boats – they are the last stronghold of the independent Captain.' Before leaving this interesting subject I think it is right to say that in the 1960s there was quite a swing back towards giving the Captain a more dignified status and more power of decision. And I believe one reason why BOAC was such a big success was that they did not impose the same rigid ground control of Captains that you saw in some other lines.

The war was now drawing to a close and this had various developments for we people operating the transport links in

Africa, India and the Middle East. The conquest of North Africa meant that the Poole-based flying boats met us in Cairo, instead of in Lagos. They used the Sunderlands to provide the link from England via Gibraltar and Jerba on the North African coast. As they did not now fly into neutral countries the Poole pilots started wearing RAF instead of BOAC uniforms. I have never quite understood why, but I think it may have made it easier for them when staying in RAF Messes. At the southern end of the route there were gradually more civilian passengers and they wanted a service which started and finished at Johannesburg. So this was now provided using the huge lake at Vaaldam, near Johannesburg. And another interesting little diversion for us was providing a service to the big island of Madagascar, recently conquered from the Vichy-French. I used to enjoy my flights in there. From Mombasa we struck out into the Indian Ocean to land at the gorgeous little French island of Pamanzi. This delightful spot was one of the centres of the perfume industry and many of the ingredients were grown here. We only used Pamanzi for refuelling and flew on from there to the huge sheltered harbour of Diego Suarez in the north of Madagascar. This big island is little known by British people. It is considerably larger than the British Isles, is mostly quite high and has a cool climate, and its people, the Malgache, are an Asian race, kin to the Malays.

We used to arrive in Diego Suarez fairly early in the day and I usually took the crew up into the hills where there was a small rest house. The country around was grassy, wooded and very pretty with wild raspberries and strawberries growing in profusion. The Malgache seemed very pleased when Britain handed over the whole administration to free France.

By now we chaps down in Durban were feeling more and more South African and less and less British. In fact the Poole-based crews swore we looked and sounded like South Africans; and if the boat from England had arrived before one of ours in Cairo when we came alongside the Nile steamer, the pale, thin lads from England would shout, 'Here come the Jaapies.' South Africa's lovely climate, huge resources and general air of being an up-and-coming country made us wonder whether we would be wise to bring our families back to England at all. So most of us, including myself, put in claims for South African citizenship.

When the war finally ended we indulged for a bit in pious hopes that the Durban boats could be kept going, by using one or two long-range boats we had, to provide a link through to England.

Unfortunately for these kinds of dreams the powers-that-be in civil aviation had really got their knives into flying boats and especially our old pre-war boats. Although we did establish the link with England and indeed I flew into Poole and out again once, it was decided to abolish our old Number 8 Line in Durban to the great sadness of all concerned. As there was little shipping available the loss of the C Class boat fleet meant that the big movement of migrants (an estimated one million British ex-servicemen wanted to emigrate to South Africa) could not take place. And this in turn caused the fall of the United Party in South Africa and their replacement by the Nationalists, with their policy of Apartheid.

At this time quite a number of my old colleagues, such as Biltong Bellin, Peter Wood, George Norris and so on, decided they would stay in South Africa and try their luck out of aviation. But Joanie and I decided, reluctantly, that we would go to Britain, and we started packing up all our belongings in 1946. It was rather amusing that just a week before we left I was standing on the step in my Durban North home when I was surprised to see a typical civil servant, dark suit, hat, brief-case and all come down the road. He turned into our gate and in a moment was spreading out some papers on the dining room table:

'Mr Fry,' he beamed at me, 'I'm from the Department of Immigration. I'm delighted to inform you that you are now a South African Citizen.'

In many ways I was sorry to have to tell him that I had changed my mind and was going back to the mists, rain and post-war problems of England. And on 17th October 1946, Joanie and I, with our three children (little Susan had been born about a year earlier) and most of our worldly goods, got on board G-ADHL, Royal Mail Aircraft *Canopus*, and set off for England. The plane was packed with staff and their families so it was quite a happy, care-free flight, though I was sad at having to command the final flight of one of the first of the great Empire Boats. I realised that at the end of the voyage, the anti-boat brigade would have their way, and the grand old lady would be sold for scrap.

Incidentally, it is perhaps interesting for students of this kind of thing to note the fantastic success of the C Class fleet. They were all ordered, direct from the drawing board, by the Imperial Airways chiefs. Each one was designed for a maximum speed of 200 mph and I understand that the average achieved throughout the fleet of 30-odd machines was 199½ mph. The boats did a great job throughout the war, being as much of a resounding success as their landplane counterparts, the Armstrong Whitworth Ensigns, were a failure. Yet, instead of modernising them with up-to-date engines as was done with the Ensigns, BOAC scrapped them. On our entirely uneventful flight home in *Canopus*, although the boat was nearly ten years old, she averaged 153 mph for the flight, almost exactly the cruising speed which Short Brothers had advertised years before. There were no engineering defects whatever to report when I handed her over to the engineers at Hythe and I wrote in the Maintenance Log:

'*Canopus* handed over to the engineers at Hythe after ten magnificent years of service. There are no defects on this aircraft and it is a disgrace that she should be put to the blow-torch.'

So ended perhaps the most enjoyable period of my life. Gone was the sunshine of South Africa; gone the boats I loved so well; and Joan and Howard Fry, with Jennifer, John and (now) Susan had to get used to the cold and shortages of post-war Britain.

5

Testing and Talking

When I first brought my wife and three small children back to England from South Africa in October 1946 we were happily ignorant of the impact which cold, financial stringency and all the various shortages would have on us.

To begin with neither Joanie nor I were very fit. We both had suffered for some years from amoebic dysentery, rather a prevalent disease in South Africa. Jennifer, John and Susan were quite fit but, of course, they had been born in the warmth of South Africa and had spent their lives there. So for all of us the impact of temperatures of 35 or 40 degrees F was fairly devastating. We reckoned the children had to have at least one walk every day, and I can still see in my mind's eye the sad little caravan of two adults and three sunburnt children actually crying with the cold as they wandered along the front in Bournemouth.

Fortunately, I had found a new job with the equally new Development Flight at Hurn, near Bournemouth, which wanted a pilot who flew both flying boats and landplanes.

The billeting officer there presumably thought that Captains were as rich as Croesus, and had booked the Fry family into the Linden Hall Hydro, an immense and very luxurious establishment with an indoor swimming pool and a squash court. To begin with we swanned about in this classy establishment feeling that BOAC would not have put us there if it was beyond our means. Then one day Mr Foss, the Director, asked me into his office:

'Mr Fry, I don't wish to pry into your affairs but I think you should know that your bill here is likely to come to more than your total income after tax.'

'But, good heavens, isn't there any special rate for BOAC? Or surely, they must contribute something towards the bill?'

'There's nothing at all like that, I assure you. In fact, I just cannot imagine why they sent you here at all.'

'Well, it's certainly very kind of you to explain it all to me.'

'Well, not all businessmen are sharks, you know. And anyway my company would be quite willing to give you a special rate whilst you are looking for a furnished flat.'

Meanwhile, I had got down to my new job without delay. First of all I had to convert yet again, back to landplanes. This involved a stay at the BOAC Training School at Aldermaston in Berkshire, where I did an SBA Course. SBA was the latest thing at the time in blind landing aids for landplanes. In effect it was a much more localised and accurate form of radio range and with much blood, sweat and tears, it did bring you to the end of the runway. I could not help contrasting all the concentration and effort with the ease with which, some time before, I had landed in fog on the water at Beira. There I had merely come over the beacon on a course which I knew would take me over the wide expanse of the landing area and then bring the plane gently down until the hull softly kissed the surface of the water.

On getting back to Hurn, I assumed my new duties as a Test Pilot with BOAC's Technical Development Department. Our job was to test new aircraft and items of equipment which it was thought might be useful to the Airline. We mounted the equipment on our two work-horses, an old Lancaster Victor Nan and a Liberator, still sporting roundels and its RAF number 632. Dennis Satchwell, who I was destined to see throughout my flying life in various jobs, taught me to fly the Lanc, always a lovely machine, and Gertie Garside gave me dual on the Lib, a real old flying lorry of a plane. Gertie was rather surprised when, harking back to boat days, I tried to use

81

differential throttle to keep the Lib straight on landing. Differential brake was the right thing, as he told me with his usual vigour.

Our performance-testing duties were on landplanes and flying boats so we really had a very varied life. As soon as I had learnt to fly the Lanc I was off to Number 4 Line at Hythe, which was just introducing its smart new post-war flying boats. These were really only civilianised versions of the Hercules-engined Sunderland 4 and the twin Wasp-engined Sunderland 5. But they were certainly very attractive machines, with proper bars, the big interior split up into little cabins, and in the roof-space a sleeping compartment, which passengers took it in turns to use. This had mattresses on the floor and rejoiced in the name of 'Annie's room'.

Both were nice aeroplanes to fly, with an impressive surge of power on take-off, when you compared them with the Pegasus-engined boats. As our performance testing showed us, the Solent would cruise along at 190 mph, with 40 passengers, while the Plymouth took 35 along at an easy 170 mph. These were not bad speeds and certainly meant that the boats were better all-round machines than the Yorks and Lancastrians which Number 2 Line, the landplane outfit, were flying.

These were quite exciting days because new autopilots, flight systems, landing aids and navigation systems were coming out all the time. We had a very big test programme to cope with it all. The Liberator soon vanished as being rather expensive and uncomfortable and we put early ILS sets into a Dove, and the excellent Smith's Auto Pilot into a Viking.

A bi-product of the experiences which we soon noticed was that ordinary Line Pilots had an over-hopeful idea of the performance you could expect from those post-war planes. Although the Lancaster was a splendid plane and it was a pleasure to fly it, the civil plane based on the Lanc, the York, was rather a cow of an aircraft and not much fun to fly. We checked the York's performance carefully and it flew exactly as the manual predicted. But the Line Pilots expected a better climb and a more impressive three-engine performance. The same applied to the Plymouth, which was really a tarted-up and faired-off version of the Sunderland 5, with its Twin Wasp engines. We carried out tropical trials of this 'boat' at Bahrain; and although the Line Pilots were disappointed we found the aircraft did just what the makers said it would. We found the Solent 'boat' to be quite a pleasant aeroplane although some of the older 'boat' pilots thought it had too high an approach speed. What we had to admit was that the Solent did not quite produce the 200 mph which Shorts claimed. We thought this was partly because it had rather ugly wing-tip floats and when Shorts built a Mark Two Solent with neater floats and engine fairings this did in fact achieve the 200 mph cruising speed the makers claimed. But the improved 'boats' were only operated by the New Zealanders on the service to Auckland.

Nevertheless, there were pleasant trips offering compensations. One was to carry out tropical trials on the Vickers Viking. This was to become the standard airliner for British European Airways and we flew it out of Negombo Aerodrome in Ceylon. It was really quite a good machine and we were glad to recommend it for BEA use. One of our last jobs was to fly the Hermes Airliner which was to be used on the popular route to Johannesburg. The Hermes, which was developed from the Halifax Bomber, was a much nicer plane than the old York, but it suffered from the fact that the Bristol Hercules engines did not deliver the power the makers advertised. I was never fond of just flying according to the book (that is the Instruction Manual), and I found in the Hermes that if you flew it in Weak Mixture, you just could not get enough power. So I flew in Rich Mixture with 2000 revolutions per minute instead of Weak Mixture and 2300 rpm. The funny thing was that my system gave me more speed and a higher operating height than the book figures. And I was to prove this thoroughly when Development Flight was wound up and we all went back to ordinary line flying.

As I have already mentioned, perhaps one of the silliest things BOAC ever did was to give up flying boats and thus to abandon the plans to operate the latest 'boat', the giant Saunders Roe Princess. We were particularly disappointed in Development Flight because the big 'boat' would have come

83

to us first. Again, a lot of people perhaps have forgotten the plane which would have become Britain's first Jumbo. Just to refresh everyone's memory the Princess flew along the runway for the Farnborough Air Show at 400 mph two years running. And again, so that we all know what we are talking about, we were in touch with the pilots who flew the Princess on its maker's trials and they confirmed that the plane was one of the first ever to exceed its designer's figures. Furthermore, there wasn't just one Princess built; there were three of these magnificent planes. And at a time when BOAC landed twice on the way to New York, the Princess could have flown this, the most important air route in the world, in just 12 hours non-stop. As an alternative, the Princess, when fitted with Rolls-Royce jet engines, could have replaced no less than 13 land-planes on African services. In the process it would have cut the journey time to all destinations and reduced the fares. The big flying boats did not use the old-fashioned system of Control Launches and Passenger Launches. Saunders Roe had designed an automatic flying boat dock. All the Captain had to do was to taxi between two pairs of buoys; two lines would make contact with snap-hooks on the bottom of the hull and electric motors ashore would have drawn the 'boat' into the dock. And we were no longer talking of the 75 or so passengers we used to carry in those old days. The Princesses could have carried anything from 100 passengers in super luxury, with a separate bar and dining room, to 250 passengers in today's style. Another misconception was that the Princesses could not have operated from London. But the Chairman of the Port of London Authority wrote to us to say that he would be pleased to open Limehouse Reach to BOAC for flying boat operation. So we could perhaps have had a different system of airline flying with a much bigger role for Britain even though flying boats could never have flown in the winter to such important cities as Moscow and Montreal.

Although, frankly, it never seemed to me that there was enough work to go round for we BOAC Test Pilots, I quite enjoyed the flying I did do. One day it might mean flying the Chairman, Sir Miles Thomas, somewhere in the tiny little

Miles Gemini. Another day I would be taking up a big four-engined York for performance testing. And then perhaps I would be off to Hong Kong as co-pilot on a Plymouth Flying Boat, just in order to keep my hand in on route flying and boat-handling.

One or two interesting trips included the tropical trials of the Smith's Auto Pilot, the latest in automatic sextants and Marconi's newest Automatic Direction Finder. All this work was done at Ratmalana in Ceylon on our old Viking G-AGRR. Not only did I find it fun to fly out East on landplanes, because, of course, I had only been there on boats before, but our two weeks or so in Ceylon were quite interesting. The island had just been made an independent member of the Commonwealth and all was hope for the future. The old pro-British Leader, Senanayake, was in power; many British Civil Servants were still at their posts; and cleanliness and law and order, Raj-style, still prevailed.

6

Back on the Routes Again

The first few years after the war were a sort of cloud-cuckoo time in civil aviation. The old try-to-pay-dividends attitude of Imperial Airways had been succeeded by some mad-cap spending. But it soon became clear that air transport would have to pay its way. So the dead wood had to be cut away. One of the first branches of BOAC to feel the axe was the little outfit – Technical Development – for which I was working. Although, as the pilots' spokesman on the National Joint Council at Hurn Airport, I did my best to save the jobs of the pilots, engineers and office staff involved, Ernest Hessey, Manager at Hurn, decreed that we would be cut down to almost nothing. The pilots would have to be absorbed elsewhere. Personally, I had no trouble. As one of those involved with the testing and acceptance of the new Handley Page Hermes Airliners, I was an automatic choice for flying them down the routes. And after going through some route familiarisation trips I took Hermes G-ALDJ down to Lagos and back. So my days as a Test Pilot were over and I was back as an ordinary Route Captain.

Nevertheless it was quite a milestone in British aviation history when we started to fly from Heathrow. Just 12 miles from London it had recently been a nice level piece of country, mostly used by market gardeners who grew vegetables there for London. Naturally, the very fine runways were built long

86

before there were any car parks for the pilots who flew from there. What it amounted to was that we just had to drive to the airport and leave our cars for a week or so on the open ground by the Bath Road. The temptation was, I am afraid, far too much for local thieves and they just could not leave the crews' cars alone. In fact, the airport soon got the name of Thief Row. Captains would come home from a trip and find no wheels on their cars. And the worst case was when a skipper came from a trip to Johannesburg to find someone had taken the engine out of his car! The only answer was to have a car which was so unpopular that no one would either steal it or steal things off it. So I bought myself a car which I really did not like at all. It was a Bond three-wheeler with a noisy 250cc Villiers engine and I bought a heavy canvass cover to fit over it. I'm pleased to say that no one ever stole anything from the car. And really its cruising speed of 45 mph was quite suitable for the 35 miles to the Heathrow area from Goring, where my family had moved to.

I am afraid that in this early post-war period the aircraft builders did not supply BOAC with very good machines. The Solent flying boat, on which I had done some of the performance testing, was a good ten mph below the maker's expected performance of 200 mph cruising speed, and this, no doubt, was one of the reasons why the Solent services to Nairobi and Johannesburg introduced with such hope in 1948 were replaced by Hermes services in 1950 as the standard BOAC plane.

But the Hermes itself was very disappointing in performance. Instead of the 240 mph which we had expected, this apparently well-streamlined aircraft only cruised at about 210 mph and in the tropics it sometimes only made around 200 mph. One of the main problems was the Hercules engine. This had been boosted up to give 2,100 hp for take-off, but it would not deliver much more than half this when set for economical cruise. So although it sailed off the ground fairly effortlessly and climbed well up to 13 or 14,000 ft, when you tried to level it off, with about 1,050 hp set up, it just fell out of the sky. Sometimes in Africa, I would have to climb it up to the required altitude, and then trim it down for level flight, three times before it finally just managed to hold its height. Of course, the only two ways of operating it were either to fly with the nose up the whole time, just to maintain height, or to forget the instructions on the power to be used and simply cram on enough power to get a decent performance.

The problem with the Hermes was that it was designed as a tail-wheel aircraft and then altered to use a nose-wheel. As a result it was too heavy and had a poor performance. I used to fly on the route to Nairobi for example. And although the Hermes could take-off and climb from Nairobi it just would not cruise at the 17,000 feet which BOAC Operations called for. As a former Development Pilot I used to cruise in Rich Mixture. I found the Hercules would produce quite enough power then for cruising at relatively high altitudes. But, of course, going against the book always has its problems. Those were the days when the BOAC Management was trying to cut the pilots down to size so that Captains who ignored the regulations and used higher powers became very unpopular.

One day when I was dead-heading (flying as a passenger) Sir Miles Thomas asked whether I had figures to prove that my policy of flying in Rich Mixture was better than the book policy of struggling to keep the plane going in Weak Mixture. Luckily, I sent my figures to Sir Miles and I heard no more about the controversy. How the other Captains flew the Hermes I have no idea, but the Hermes went on dragging its tail through the air routes of the world. Passengers called it 'the ship' that never reaches the top of the climb. I contend, I had proved quite conclusively that the maximum power in Weak Mixture Cruise was not enough to get any kind of satisfactory performance and that using Rich Mixture Cruise could get a good speed (say 220 mph), a nice level altitude, a cooler engine and just as good a range.

We also flew the Hermes on the route to Johannesburg and we found it rather unpopular. BOAC had first of all run the service with the Solent and it had been operated as a sort of air cruise with nights spent ashore at attractive places like Victoria Falls. And passengers did not like the change to a rather dull landplane which flew right through the night. The South African Government did their best to keep the Solent service; they even offered to pay the expenses for the flying boat base at Vaaldam so that BOAC would only have to pay a landing fee. But BOAC were determined to stop the flying boats and go over to landplanes. This was perhaps a mistake at the time, because the Americans built the best land airliners, whereas Britain built by far the best 'boats'.

In those old days the new Jan Smuts Airport had not been built and the Hermes Service to Johannesburg used a short, narrow field called Palmietfontein. It was not dangerous, or BOAC would not have used it. But it was not a good field from the pilot's point of view.

The Hermes was also used to fly the other African service to Lagos and Accra. It was not much of a problem on that service because the landings were mostly at or near sea-level. But Britain was not very competitive. On the Eastern Routes BOAC was using a Canadian version of a well known American plane. This was the DC4M4 christened the Argonaut by BOAC. It was actually a Douglas DC4 fitted with Merlin engines and a pressure cabin and except for the noise it was a better plane than the Hermes. It cruised at around 240 mph as against the 220 on the Hermes.

This was a period when all sorts of new British Airliners were in course of construction. They were:

The Bristol Britannia, a 350 mph airliner seating up to 100 passengers

The Bristol Brabazon, a 330 mph airliner seating up to 150 passengers

The De Havilland Comet, a 500 mph airliner seating up to 80 passengers

The Saunders Roe Princess, a 360 mph flying boat seating up to 200 passengers

As readers will have gathered, I had always been keen on flying boats and on British aircraft. This, of course, made me unpopular with Whitney Straight, BOAC's half-American Chief Executive. His policy was to get BOAC operating an all-American (or Canadian) fleet of landplanes as soon as possible. To this end any suggestion that flying boats were still a good means of transport had to be kept out of the press. I wrote an article for *The Log*, the organ of the British Airline Pilots' Association, suggesting that BOAC ought to declare its enthusiastic support for those two early 'jumbos', the Brabazon and the Princess, and try to get them pressed forward as fast as possible, if necessary at the cost of delaying the Britannia a little. My argument, which everyone has now come to accept, was that, because even the largest aircraft only needs one crew, one maintenance team and one traffic team, the cost per seat mile on the big plane would always be lower than on the small one. The fact that the 'jumbo' also provided more comfort and better catering and toilet facilities was an added advantage.

Mr Straight refused to allow me to publish my article, although as I pointed out, if my reasoning was at fault the columns of the press and the aviation press were wide open for him to 'shoot me down'. My argument for keeping the Princess in the picture was a simple one. The cost to the British taxpayer, I insisted, of flying boats, plus almost free flying boat bases, was much lower than the cost of landplanes, plus the enormously expensive airports. Furthermore, as Britain was the world's leading nation for flying boat construction and America the leader in landplanes, it seemed odd to go over entirely to landplanes. Finally, if we used boats for Commonwealth communications our competitors would either have to buy boats too or spend their money, instead of ours, on building the enormous new airports all over Asia and Africa.

My arguments did not prevail. BOAC closed down the flying boat operation in 1950 and seemed to be doing their best to get rid of the Saunders Roe Princess, and the Bristol Brabazon. As far as British machines were concerned they were only interested in the Comet and the Britannia. But all four machines were being built. And all appeared at about the same time.

In contrast to the Princess's top performance at the Farnborough Air Show in the early 1950s, the Britannia was in

aptain Fry and crew 'C' Class flying boat - Johannesburg - Southampton 1946

Courtesy: Natal Daily News

ptain Fry and chief engineer (BOAC America)

Empire flying boat S23 'C' Class with passengers boarding at Southampton

Short 'C' Class flying boat, Imperial Airways and BOAC

Holiday-makers watch the launch of the Saunders Roe SR 45 'Princess' on slipway at Cowes, Isle of Wight. 200 passengers; 400 miles per hour

Courtesy: BBC Hulton Picture Library

Saunders Roe Princess in flight

Courtesy: British Hovercraft Corporation, Isle of Wight

Britannia 312 1957-1965; 380 miles an hour, London - New York non-stop

Courtesy: Adrian Meredith Aviation Librar

Boeing 707 - BOAC; 580 miles an hour, London - New York non-stop

Courtesy: Adrian Meredith Aviation Librar

trouble and its performance was not impressive. Instead of sweeping around Farnborough at high speed it crept around at very modest speeds and there were hints that the servo-tab type controls (which control the movement of the aircraft) were not working well. The problem was that all three British machines made use of the Bristol Proteus engine. This again was in short supply and was only providing about 70 per cent of the power the makers had promised. The poor old Brabazon was never actually fitted with Proteus engines at all. It flew, very slowly of course, with eight Centaurus piston engines, and was officially abandoned before it had even been tried with the right engines. This, I thought, was certainly an odd way to waste the tax-payer's money. Saunders Roe were supplied with early Proteus engines but these were not only low in power, they were also unreliable. So the test programme of the Princess was held up through engine problems. Yet the impression was left with the public (and people like me were forbidden to change it) that the Princess was rather a failure, whereas the failure was not in the plane but in its Bristol engines.

It was at this time, in 1951 and 1952, that I decided to make a last effort to get the Princess into service with BOAC. I therefore sent a twelve-page paper on the subject to Sir Miles Thomas. In it I put forward two complete plans for the use of the three boats, which had been built at a cost of £14 million. The first was to equip the Princesses with the latest 700 series Bristol Proteus engines and use them to operate a daily service between Southampton and New York. As the Princesses would have been able to do the flight in a maximum of twelve hours and could have carried the then huge total of 125 passengers and baggage I calculated that a fare of £80 could have been charged. Of course, in view of the fact that people like Whitney Straight and Sir Victor Tait were so opposed to flying boats I had to propose that the flying boat line should operate quite separately from the rest of BOAC. This would have had the advantage that maintenance could have been contracted out to Saunders Roe instead of being done, very expensively, by BOAC. And the then crazy level of ground staffing could have been avoided at the two flying boat bases.

My second plan was to equip the three boats with pure jet Rolls-Royce Avon engines and fly them on African services serving Lagos, Salisbury, Johannesburg and Nairobi. This jet version of the Princess was perfectly practicable and had, in fact, already been suggested by Saunders Roe, the aircraft's builders. They would really have sooner seen the aircraft go into service with pure jet engines which were able to give it the following excellent performance:

All Up Weight 360,000 lbs
Passenger Load 250
Additional freight and mail 10,000 lbs
Range with this payload 3,000 miles
Cruising Speed 416 mph

The plan I put forward to Sir Miles Thomas for operating the Princesses as pure jet machines was comprehensive. I included timetables for a twice-weekly service to Lagos and to Nairobi, a weekly service to Johannesburg and to Salisbury. All this could have been done with two aircraft, leaving the third either on maintenance or as a standby. The use of the three big boats in Africa would have enabled BOAC to replace the fifteen Hermes and three Comet One aircraft then in use. They would also have been able to replace the forty landplane crews by a mere eight flying boat crews.

There were further advantages to the plan. The three big boats would have actually offered more seats per week than the eighteen landplanes they would have replaced. And as their running costs per seat mile would have been so much lower the following remarkable fare reductions could have been made:

Johannesburg reduced from £315 to £200 return
Lagos reduced from £203 to £120 return
Nairobi reduced from £252 to £150 return
Salisbury reduced from £295 to £185 return

In my paper to Sir Miles I also pointed out the advantages of using flying boats for the still larger aircraft of the future. It would have been entirely practicable to have the three Princesses in operation on either of the schemes I suggested by 1956. So Britain would have been operating 'jumbos' with all their

92

known advantages about ten years before the Americans could have produced the 747 on the routes. But I also looked forward to the introduction by the early Sixties of 550 mph Delta Wing flying boats using the Olympus engine, which now powers the Concorde. Naturally, my paper pointed out that the longer runways needed for these faster, and perhaps noisier aircraft, would cost virtually nothing, if they were flying boats, and they would likewise cause no noise nuisance, except perhaps to the fish and the seagulls!

Sir Miles reacted with the courtesy and efficiency which made him such a popular Chairman. He first of all acknowledged the receipt of my paper and then promised a full reply when he had studied my proposals in detail. Finally, a month later, I was very happy to get Sir Miles' full reply, which was highly satisfactory to me. In it he said: 'The Board of the Corporation have now decided to ask the Ministry of Civil Aviation to allow us to operate the Princess, on the basis of the aircraft remaining in Air Ministry ownership.' He also went on to say that my paper had helped in developing his own ideas on the subject and he thanked me for my work.

It is natural, I accept, that I should have felt pretty pleased with the way things now looked like developing. Not only did I have an excellent chance of flying the biggest and one of the fastest planes in the world; but at least there was a possibility that I might secure some kind of administrative post with the new Flying Boat Division. Sir Miles Thomas had told me to expect an announcement in the press about the introduction of the big flying boats and for months I scanned the aviation press for any word about it. But nothing whatever was said. And I still have no idea why Sir Miles and the Board of BOAC changed their minds. I remain convinced that whatever their reasons for turning the Princesses down, they made a bad mistake. Especially as the landplanes they operated instead all turned out to be quite a disappointment. I refer, particularly, to the ill-fated Comet One, withdrawn only a short time after its introduction and the Britannia, which had appalling teething troubles for a couple of years after it first appeared, and the

Stratocruiser, which although popular with Atlantic passengers failed to make a profit.

Once my efforts on behalf of flying boats had failed I just settled down to enjoying the very pleasant job of being an aircraft Captain. Until the end of 1952 I was still peddling the slow, old Hermes around the routes and trying to make the best of it. Then in the Spring of 1953 I was rather excited to have the opportunity of a period on the Comet One. This aeroplane was the most fantastic leap forward in aviation and it is an appalling tragedy that BOAC had to give the machine up after a series of unexplained crashes. Personally, I think De Havilland did a wonderful job in putting a 500 mph jetliner in service in 1952 and I do not think they can be blamed for the one small design fault which caused the plane to be grounded. But I do feel strongly that the Government of the day showed unbelievable timidity and incompetence in taking so long to get the successor, the Comet Four, out on the routes. I blame the Government for allowing the American Boeing company to catch Britain up at this crucial time, because it was the politicians who could have produced the really big money needed to have got the Comet Four out in 1955 or 1956, rather than the fairly small De Havilland Company. It is all history now but what a display of bumbling incompetence it was which put the Comet on the Atlantic only a matter of months before the far superior Boeing 707 appeared.

But Britain was still trying to compete in the 'big league'. Take our first effort, the De Havilland Comet One. The trouble really was that aircraft designers had not found out about the problems with flying at heights such as 40,000 feet or those associated with taking off with a jet airliner.

I am not a great authority on the Comet One because I only flew it for a short time. But it was certainly rather an attractive plane after the Hermes. It had much more effective flaps and brakes and it was a far more comfortable plane than the Hermes for operations at Palmietfontein (Johannesburg). It was quite easy to get in and out of this field, although it was on the short side. But in general, pilots were not very confident about the plane. Although its cruising speed of 500 miles an hour was a tremendous advance on the 250 mph of the day, it did suffer from a lot of accidents and until the plane was withdrawn the cause of these accidents was just not known. My friend Maurice Haddon lost his life flying at 40,000 feet or so and another friend of mine, Charles Pentland, crashed after take-off in Karachi. At the time the authorities did not know the cause of either accident. But we now know that high altitude crashes were the result of the fact that the crew escape hatch in the cockpit had square corners instead of being circular or nearly circular; and we now know square or oblong hatches simply could not stand the pressure differential which results from flying at 40,000 feet. As to take-off and climb accidents, these apparently resulted from easing the Comet off the ground before the De Havilland Ghost engines had developed their full power. Charles Pentland was an excellent pilot on post-war piston planes like the Lockheed Constellation. But we now know that, although when you were taking off in a Constellation you eased it off the ground as soon as you reached a safe speed, with a Comet it was quite different. You had to keep it hammering away along the runway until the jet engines developed their full power; and then you had plenty of power for the climb out. Pentland did not realise it, I am sure, but he pulled his Comet off too soon and he never got full climb power.

It is easy to be wise after the event but I still think the British authorities committed a fatal error by taking so long to solve the problems of the Comet One. The final Comet, the Comet Four, was an excellent plane but it was not nearly as good a jetliner as the Boeing 707 and, as has been noted, it only came on the routes just before the Boeing. Britain should have put more men and more money on the Comet problem very much sooner. It is surely quite obvious that if Britain could have offered a practical jetliner a full year before America brought one out, we would have been the world's leaders in airliner design and we would have secured hundreds of orders. But we have to accept the facts as they were and BOAC withdrew the Comet and its routes had to be handed over to the Argonaut. So for some years I was an Argonaut pilot.

Although a clever improvement on the old Douglas DC4 (speed up from 180 to 230, operating height up from 10,000 to 18,000) the Canadian-built Argonaut was a depressing aircraft to fly after the Comet. Although faster and more reliable than the Hermes, it was darker, more cramped and very noisy. And, naturally, it did not in any way compare with the Comet. Although, as I explained, my Comet experience was limited, I had very much enjoyed flying this amazingly advanced aeroplane. One amusing incident sticks in my mind. In April 1953 I was flying Comet GALYS on a trip to Johannesburg. At Khartoum I met two RAF Officers flying a pair of Vampires down to Salisbury. They had never seen a Comet before and were rather condescending about it:

'Well, skipper, we'll be off now. Don't suppose we'll see you again. We should just about be finished refuelling by the time you taxi in at Entebbe.'

Pete Worrell, my First Officer at the time, and I kept very quiet about the Comet's excellent performance. But we had arranged to have the passengers marshalled and ready to go. So the moment the two Vampires taxied out we put everyone on board and we were off only a few minutes after them. It must have been a couple of very surprised RAF types who saw a Comet come surging past them before they even reached the top of the climb.

Basically though, during the late Fifties I was ploughing around the African air routes in the old Argonaut. We went to Nairobi through Rome, Cairo, Khartoum and Entebbe. And we also went down to Johannesburg with a call at Livingstone and we kept our familiarity with West Africa by flying to Tripoli, Kano, Lagos and Accra. I cannot say it was a great deal of fun. We had to keep the engine power down, partly because the Rolls Merlin engines, though they had plenty of power, were rather noisy. Also, as they had been designed for the Air Force, they did not like low power very much. So after they had been flown at Cruise Power for some time they became rather unreliable, and for the only time with an airliner we had to give the plane full power for a few minutes. It was quite fun to feel the old planes get their noses down and surge forward. But as the years went by we were more and more aware that we were flying an old-fashioned and not very popular plane. It was also rather depressing to find that the Argonaut was steadily getting slower and slower. Although it was a good idea to begin with to give the old DC4 more power, in later years it became clear that the plane could not keep up the 240 mph the Merlins gave it originally. In fact its cruising speed dropped to around 220 mph.

7

British and Best on Britannias

I settled down to some fairly dull flying. It was the old routine of trips on the noisy old Argonaut to East Africa, West Africa and South Africa. We did our best to keep the passengers happy with good food, pretty, attentive stewardesses and, in my case, anyway, visits by the Captain to chat up the customers and show them where they were on the map. Some of us also got BBC news bulletins and distributed them around.

In truth this was to make up for the fact that we had a noisy, slow, old-fashioned aeroplane; and I cannot really claim that the passengers liked the Argonaut much. We pilots had the feeling that we were just marking time until something better turned up. And indeed we were. The machine we were waiting for was the very overdue Britannia. More about that on-again-off-again machine later on.

But to return to the mundane business of airliners. As I explained in an earlier chapter those early 'jumbos', the Princess Flying Boats, were competitors with the Britannia airliner for the quite advanced gas-turbine engine, the Bristol Proteus. BOAC's anti-flying-boat management had insisted that the first fully developed Proteus engines were to go to the Britannias. And that, in effect, signed the death warrant for the Princess, which was never able to show its paces with a fully rated engine. But instead of Britannias coming rushing out of the Bristol factory and on to the BOAC routes, there was nothing but trouble.

First of all, the Filton workforce behaved as though next week, next month or next year would do just as well. And they seemed quite unmoved by the news of huge orders from America if the Britannia could be got out on routes quickly. Every now and again we Captains would visit Filton to see how things were going, but it was a torment to see the snail's pace at which the machines were being built.

At the end of one visit, the Bristol works manager asked us what we thought of things. We said, 'We've never seen men work so slowly', and with that the union shop steward bustled up and said: 'Any more of that sort of talk and I'll blow my whistle and call every one out'. It was this sort of union attitude which did the British aircraft industry so much harm. And it was partly responsible for the fact that the American firm TWA eventually cancelled an order for some 50 Britannias.

Additionally, people have suggested that the unbelievable complication of the electrical system was simply a result of trying to give everyone in the electrics side of the industry some of the action – and the gravy. And I think there is no doubt that the use of American electrics and cabin pressurisation would have got the aircraft out quicker.

Then, the Proteus engine had really been designed for the Princesses and the Brabazons, on which it would have been mounted warmly in the wing. In the Britannia it was hung out in the airflow, where its vulnerable, reverse-flow design caused it to ice up. I remember once on a proving flight in Africa we were amazed to hear the high powered Bristol engineer on board say:

'You BOAC pilots are just making a fuss about nothing. These engines don't stop through ice very often. And if they do, well you just relight them'.

I decided we just had to make him face facts. So when we took a party of the engineers for a flight down Africa I flew the Britannia on purpose right into the middle of a big rain storm. I should explain that I happened to be the Captain on duty at the

99

time and that the Britannia was fitted with an excellent radar set just next to the Captain's seat. When I swung the plane round towards the storm (shown as a bright yellow blob on the radar screen) the duty Bristol engineer said: 'Surely, Captain, you are not going to fly through that?' I told him that I certainly was. And in we went. Within five minutes all four engines had stopped in turn and been restarted by our very efficient Flight Engineer, Ginger Johnson. The Bristol men were suitably shaken and they worked hard to design the electric air intake heater which eventually solved the problem by keeping the engine ice-free. But the troubles had taken too long.

Finally, very gingerly, at the end of 1956 we did start to use the Britannia for trooping flights. And in February 1957 the 'Whispering Giant' as the publicity boys called it, was at last in full operation on African services. But Britain and Bristol's had missed the bus, as far as the enormously important American internal market was concerned. Airlines like TWA decided that although they would have liked the quiet and the 340mph speed of the Britannia, they could not afford the risk of a lot of electrical trouble and the occasional engine flaming out in icing conditions. So they stuck to the 300mph DC7C, a reliable work-horse of a plane, although it was noisy and slow.

Personally, I always rather liked the Britannia from the start. It had an absolutely effortless performance on take-off, and on landing the effect of putting the huge airscrews into reverse power on two engines was quite impressive. It gave you a nice comfortable feeling to know that you could pull up amazingly quickly if you really had to. And most of the 'snags' on the machine were finally cured. Using Brits down Africa, BOAC began to get back the popularity which they had not had since the Comet days. And South African Airways, who had been riding pretty high with their Douglas planes, now saw the traffic flowing back to us. Quite apart from being faster than the DC6Bs, DC7s and DC7Cs the Brits were quieter and roomier and they were able to fly a bit higher. And this is very important in a bumpy old continent like Africa.

As one of the first people to fly the Britannia down the

routes, I was now busy in 1957 checking out other Argonaut pilots as African Route Captains on Brits. This work was normally pleasant and not too demanding because I was dealing with highly trained and very efficient people. But one trip was extraordinary. Norman, an old chum of mine, did several very mediocre approaches and landings on our way to Johannesburg. But his arrival at Jan Smuts Airport down there, was quite an event.

To begin with, Norman was at least a couple of thousand feet too high at Hartebeestepoort Beacon, as the Ground Controller tersely told him. And he crossed the boundary of the enormous Jan Smuts main runway so high and fast that we used the whole of two miles of runway – the longest, incidentally, in Africa.

'Can I have the pilot's name please?' said the Controller, 'I've never seen anything like that in my life. In fact, man, if I hadn't seen it I wouldn't have bloody believed it.'

When we got into the old Langham Hotel in the centre of the business area of Johannesburg I just had to ask Norman why on earth his approach and landing at Jan Smuts had been so very odd.

'Well, Howard,' he said with some embarrassment, 'the fact is, that I have done this course on how to write novels and I was just working out in my mind the plot for my next story.'

'Well, for God's sake, Norman, do compose the damn things in your spare time or you'll never make a Britannia skipper.'

In a world which had rather forgotten the quick rise and fall of the ill-fated Comet, the Britannia was now getting to be quite a sensation. Its effortless starting, without the popping and banging you get on piston engines, its amazing silence at airports and the near 400mph speed, which was now being achieved on the bigger Britannia 312, combined to make BOAC feel the time had come to put the machine on the Atlantic. And this, in turn, meant that we Britannia Captains were going to be able to break into the exclusive North Atlantic Union, hitherto the jealously guarded preserve of a small group of pilots who had flown the 'pond' since the war-time days of Liberators and Boeing Clippers.

So I found myself in May 1957 attached to the Stratocruiser Fleet for some North Atlantic experience. It was all very new to me and quite good fun. Of course the 'Strat', as it was called, was slow and noisy compared with the Brit. But its huge cockpit, its crew rest-bunks, and its doubledeck layout, with the very attractive downstairs bar, made it rather a remarkable machine. The Strat took an incredibly long time to get to New York – my first trip was 10 hours and 6 minutes to Gander in Newfoundland plus a further 4 hours and 36 minutes on to New York. The bumping about at low altitude, the constant pounding of the big piston engines certainly combined to make the Atlantic crossing of 1957 a damn tiring affair and I could well understand the insistence of the Pilots' Association that we must have a minimum of two days in New York before flying home. As one of the old boat-hands who had tried to maintain the status of Captains I was pleased to see that North Atlantic skippers were treated with proper respect. The crew and the ground staff at all stations did their utmost to provide everything the skippers might want and no one questioned their right to make all their own decisions.

The poor old Britannia was still getting trouble with engines flaming out and it was not until November, when we had got heated inductions and really fool-proof automatic relighting of engines that, under the watchful eye of Don Anderson, one of the Atlantic old-timers, we started to get the Britannias into regular Atlantic route service.

Andy, as he was called, was a dour Scot and his motto was, 'Ye canna be too careful'. And in many ways they were wise sentiments. The Atlantic weather is tricky; the distances are great; you need a quick, decisive mind to deal with the emergencies which may arrive; and you really need to know all about the various airports you use.

But one day it all backfired. As we came past Gander on a London/New York flight we received a report of a bad snow storm down there. 'Ye canna be too careful,' said Anderson and he decided to land at Gander and wait until the snow had cleared. It was rather a mistake because as we came into land the Britannia flew into freezing rain. The dangerous stuff coated the plane so badly that we had to put it into a hangar and clear it with jets of hot air. We were delayed for hours and maybe we learnt the lesson that 'you can indeed be too careful'!

Andy was quite right, though, to see that we all knew our way in and out of Washington, Boston, Montreal, Goose Bay and Gander. But that done, in my opinion at any rate, he could have started a full service to New York, and done much of the training on the route. But instead of that there were months and months of training flights, sometimes three of them per week with a whole mass of crew members on board and, of course, no passengers. And as for route flights with passengers, for months we only flew one service a week to and from New York. So huge sums were being spent on training, and almost nothing was being earned on the few route flights.

I was one of the first Brit pilots to be passed out on the Atlantic and, indeed, I operated the second Britannia Atlantic Service on the 26th December 1957. It sticks in my mind because just 300 miles East of Gander one of the engines failed. The operations manual said clearly that in such a case I must land at the nearest airport. My Engineer Officer naturally pointed this out to me and asked my permission to start the process of getting an engine flown into Gander. I refused and told the whole crew that, in view of the publicity involved in such an early Britannia flight, I intended to fly on to New York. BOAC crew members were very 'book' minded and both the engineer and the navigator said that they intended to make a complaint and a full report to their respective chiefs when we got home. 'That's your privilege,' I said, 'but we're still going on to New York.'

The navigator, a very persistent man, then claimed we had not sufficient fuel to make New York on three engines. But I still reckoned that the adverse publicity of taking BOAC's new toy into Gander for an engine change on its second trip would be disastrous. So I pressed on. And in fact we reached New York in only thirteen hours' total time and we actually had more fuel left than we had calculated would remain at the end of a four-engined flight.

I must admit to having had some worries about how the BOAC management would react to my decision. But it is good to report that I was officially congratulated for using my initiative and saving the Corporation's public image.

So we were really pleased with ourselves and the Britannia. The long-range plane finally brought to an end the old Atlantic service with its stops on the way. When you took your New York service out of Heathrow in the days of the Boeing Clipper, you knew you would have to land at either Prestwick, Reykjavik (Iceland) or Gander (Newfoundland) and that you might have to land at all three. But with the Britannia it was different; apart from being faster and quieter (380 mph instead of 320) it had the range to get to New York's Kennedy Airport in eleven-and-a-half hours non-stop. So the Britannia not only revolutionised BOAC's flights from Heathrow to New York but we were also able to produce faster non-stop services to important North American cities like Montreal and Detroit, as well as being able to offer one-stop flights to Chicago, Toronto and San Francisco. And by providing a Britannia service to Tokyo and a Trans-Pacific service from San Francisco to Honolulu and Tokyo, we were able to provide the best round-the-world service. They were certainly great days. I used to be immensely chuffed when I was able to fly right past American or United on the much-used flight from New York to San Francisco. 'If you look through the starboard windows you can see American Airlines Seven Seas going rapidly astern.' And it gave me a thrill when I reported to Salt Lake City on my first flight across America. I gave all my flight times to the Controller on the way to San Francisco.

'Say Speedbird,' said the Controller, 'will you check those flight-times, they seem awful fast to me?' But I knew they were correct and I told him so. He asked, 'What equipment do you have up there?' and I was able to tell him:

'This is a Bristol Britannia Airliner with Bristol Proteus engines.' I think he was quite impressed.

But the management's rather anti-British stance as far as

aircraft procurement was concerned was still pretty evident. At least that is the explanation, to my way of thinking, for the very small amount of use made of the Britannia in its early days and the almost total lack of advertising for the once weekly BA 501/502 service to New York which was all we were running in the winter of 1957/58. This contrasted with the three Brit services per week in each direction being run between Lod and New York, via London, by El Al the Israeli airline and the huge volume of very effective advertising which they were putting out.

Charles Clore, the property millionaire, has always been a frequent Atlantic traveller. I carried him on one of the early Britannia flights. He was very enthusiastic about the aircraft but very caustic about BOAC's business sense at the time.

'I can't understand it, Captain Fry,' he said. 'Here's Britain with the fastest, biggest, quietest airliner in the world and what is your airline doing with it? You run just one service a week to New York. You don't advertise it at all and even your own traffic staff seem to know practically nothing about the Britannia service to New York. And in the meantime a little airline like El Al really goes to town with your own British aircraft and makes a mint of money with it.'

It was certainly difficult to find an answer and frankly I did not try. I just suggested that perhaps Mr Clore might like to write to Sir Basil Smallpeice about it. But I have no idea whether he ever did so.

However, BOAC did gradually see that they had got a pretty good machine in the Brit and we eventually replaced both the Stratocruiser and the DC7C to the great pleasure of our passengers. Soon we were flying right across the States to San Francisco and proving to TWA, United, American and the other operators that BOAC's Britannia was the fastest thing in the American skies.

Thus began one of the most interesting and satisfying periods in my career. I was flying to New York, Detroit, Chicago and San Francisco in the States; to Montreal and Toronto in Canada; down from New York to Nassau in the Bahamas and Montego Bay in Jamaica; and at the same time I was keeping my hand in on the African route by doing the odd trip to Johannesburg. Everywhere we went we had the satisfaction of knowing we were flying the biggest, fastest thing in the sky.

8

Up from Somerset to Fly 707s

In 1960 we were very lucky suddenly to get a four-month posting to Honolulu. It was just a matter of how BOAC organised the round-the-world service. There was first of all a group of crews stationed in the UK who flew eastward to Tokyo. Then there was a similar group of people who flew as far as San Francisco and Honolulu. Naturally, it was popular, partly I suppose because the Hawaiian Islands are considered to be one of the loveliest places in the world with one of the best climates. We were fortunate in having our three children at boarding schools so when we were offered the posting at very short notice, we were able to accept.

I flew quite hard but with blue skies most of the way in both directions, there was nothing at all tricky about it. The trip to Tokyo was two seven-hour legs with a brief stop for fuel at Wake Island, a very crowded American Air Force base. Wake, like Midway, had the usual 'gooney bird' problem. These big sea-birds felt a sort of affinity with aeroplanes and would love to come in and do a landing on the runway or the taxi tracks. But they were not only bad flyers, who sometimes made a complete mess-up of judging the wind and landed all in a heap, but they were also quite reluctant to get out of the way for the airliners. So 'Go around again, gooney-birds on the runway', was quite a usual message from the Control Tower. Another problem at Wake was the very crowded tarmac,

107

which often made it necessary for us to 'back' the Britannias in or out of the parking area. Although you could do this with a Brit, the nose-wheel steering was not the Brit's best feature, so it was never a pleasure to be driving the thing backwards in between big American bombers.

Japan was a surprise to me, because I was expecting a warm, colourful, romantic city. Instead, even in 1960, it was dirty, grey and industrial, with masses of honking cars and cabs. And as for the weather, it always seemed just like our own in England, with plenty of cloud and rain. As I never had more than eighteen hours in Tokyo I was unable to get out and see the countryside, but one or two of my colleagues who did get the chance were not enthusiastic.

We were always able to fly back to Honolulu non-stop, because this part of the Pacific had strong westerly winds practically 365 days in the year. We normally had five or six days at home with our wives before flying the 2,500 miles to San Francisco. This lovely city had always been a favourite of mine and I used to enjoy the three days which the timetable gave us there. Normally we would hire a car between the various members of the crew and so see a lot of the country. At various times I went up to the famous National Park at Yosemite, with its mountains, waterfalls and rushing trout streams; to the Napa Valley for the wine-tasting; and down to the lovely artists' colony at Carmel-by-the-Sea.

Before leaving Honolulu, we were able to get our three children out for a brief holiday. Although having five in our tiny flat was quite a squeeze we were pleased to see the children's delight in the new surroundings. It was quite a laugh when they first arrived. There they were at the airport looking pale, serious and British. And they nearly walked straight past their sun-tanned, brightly dressed parents, without recognising us. But they were in great form after their three-and-a-half weeks in the Pacific paradise. The local airline, Hawaiian, were very helpful and gave us staff-rate reductions for a trip to Hawaii, the 'big island', as they called it, where we spent a few days.

As an Atlantic Captain I was rather pleased that I finally

reached the best job in BOAC. This sense of being 'the best' was also reflected in other telling ways. I shall always remember my first trip to Caracas because it did demonstrate how much people in South America respected Britain. When I arrived with my crew at our hotel in Caracas I was somewhat surprised to find the Hotel Manager there to greet me.

'Nice to see you, Captain,' he said, 'and welcome to Venezuela. The keys for all the crew are ready on the Reception Desk. So all they have to do is sign the book and they can go off to their rooms.' And the room boys had gone off with the crew bags already.

'There's only one thing I want to ask,' I said, 'and that is what about that Pan-American crew sitting there waiting?'

'Oh those people,' he said, 'we don't care about them. They grind us down to the last dollar for their room rate, and do you know they even double up their stewardesses?' Now I must say that although BOAC pay was not so good as American pay in those days, our Airline did treat us all extremely well. Captains were always given a double room with private bath and all the crew received their own rooms with their own bathrooms. The Pilots' Association had just negotiated a deal whereby the crew received pay for all the meals they missed whilst they were flying the voyage. It wouldn't have been better to take the meals in the air because the crew were usually too busy to eat a full meal, but they appreciated the snacks like coffee and biscuits which the stewardess brought round. And New York, our usual evening destination, was a splendid place for keeping open to really late hours for eating. So for myself, I used to change at our New York hotel (in my day the New Western on 50th Street) and than sally forth and buy a late dinner.

So it was natural that in the spring of 1960 I should try to get on 707s, like most of the fairly senior BOAC Captains. To begin with there was some small resistance by the management, who suggested that the aircraft was tricky to fly and needed young pilots. But BALPA naturally pointed out the senior Pan-American pilots had apparently had no difficulty and the objections were dropped. Of course, the 707 Training

Captains were fairly young chaps and although they had to accept the class who came to the BOAC Training School at Cranebank in June 1960, they did comment a bit on the average age. At 47, I was one of the youngest and one of the few who did not use glasses for reading. You could not really blame the training boys for 'taking the mickey' a bit and calling us 'the bifocal lens course' and asking us whether it was true that the 'windscreens are being built with a bit of magnification in them for you old chaps with bad distance vision?'

A lot has been written in books by pilots and books about pilots to explain the awful terrors of the six-monthly check flight. And I think those who criticise pilots' rates of pay should bear in mind that ours is the only profession where you have to remain as fit, alert and competent in all relevant ways at 50 as you were at 30. And I can certainly dispel any illusions that any of those steeped-in-vinegar aviation journalists may have that the older pilots receive a kindly, understanding check ride. They get the same treatment as everyone else. So although check flights, and six-monthly medical examinations, are a recurring anxiety throughout pilots' lives, our critics should also remember that we had to submit to an even more searching check on our capabilities every three years or so when we changed over to another type of airliner. For the information of those outside aviation, pilots have to have the most intimate knowledge of the design and construction and functioning of every new aircraft they fly. The engines, the controls, the fuel, oil, water, electrical, heating, pressurisation, hydraulic and every other system must be understood in detail before you are allowed to start to fly the new plane. And an examination mark of 85 to 90 per cent is expected in all papers.

The six-monthly check was both a written and flying test, was partly in the simulator (a pretend airliner which never leaves the ground) and partly in the real airliner. To make sure that passengers' lives are not at risk, a pilot was sacked if he failed two checks running. And to make sure that personal feelings were not involved, if a pilot failed a check, he had to have his second check with a different check Captain. You would expect that mistakes were never made with something as serious as this; but one day a pilot I knew quite well failed two checks and was duly sacked. Only the Pilots' Association noticed that both check flights had been with the same check Captain. The General Secretary of the Pilots' Association went to see the Chairman of BOAC.

'We shall be pleased to see you,' he said, 'at our annual cocktail party. But I do not think you would like us to announce that we no longer have confidence in you as Chairman of BOAC!' Rough tactics, you might say, but it worked. The Captain concerned received an apology, cash settlement and the offer of reinstatement. But perhaps wisely, he transferred to another airline and made a good career, to the best of my knowledge.

Naturally with the jibes about age, those of us on the 'bifocal lens course' on 707s had to make even more than the usual effort. We mostly moved up close to Heathrow so that we could have cramming sessions together in the evenings after the concentrated day's lecturing was over. Whenever possible we tried to get into the Boeing simulator to check on the location of everything in the cockpit and to watch others flying the simulator. And I am pleased to be able to say that at the end of it all, all we 'old' characters passed the technical examinations and the forty hours or so we had as first pilot, second pilot and engineer on the simulator with flying colours.

Although I enjoyed flying the Britannia and have always believed Britain should try to continue to be a big airliner constructor, I am afraid money does talk to us all. BOAC had to accept that the Britannia, excellent aircraft though it was, was completely outclassed by the Boeing 707 Jetliner. The 707 cruised at 570 mph instead of the Britannia's 380 and it had a range of 5,500 miles as against 4,500 on the Britannia. So BOAC offered a salary of £5,000 a year for 707 Captains compared with £4,200 for the men flying the Britannia. I know the figures seem tiny compared with those ruling today; but remember that the pound bought at least twelve times as much in those old days in 1960.

111

Anyway, I decided I must stay on the top airliner so I applied for a 707 course.

'We can't give you one yet,' said the Training Department. 'Jim Percy has just gone on 707s and he is Seniority number one. You are Seniority fifteen and you can go on the next course.'

So I did a few more Britannia trips and then went down to RAF St Mawgan to learn to fly the 707. It was a memorable business in every way. First of all it was my introduction to the very latest airliner and also I saw one of the RAF's best airfields for the first time.

I shall never forget that my instructor, Captain Rodley, when I was first introduced to my new 'mount' said: 'This is a lovely aeroplane, Howard, and you will enjoy flying it.' And taking everything together I did. 'Rod' as we called him said: 'The best way to learn about the 707 is to fly it.' So I did a circuit and then landed on the long wide runway.

'Nice landing, Howard,' said Rodley, 'but we don't fly them like that.' And he demonstrated the new technique by putting the machine down firmly in the first 100 yards of the runway. There is no doubt that with big machines like the new Boeings it is better to use rather a small amount of runway. A really lovely landing is less important. Though I discovered for myself later that if you use the 'Qantas method' landing (over-rotate and then push the stick forward until the plane lands) you get a short run and a smooth touch-down. St Mawgan has both good approaches and a well-calibrated ILS (Instrument Landing System). So we quite enjoyed practising ILS landings both by day and by night. These inevitably reminded me of the Britannia which was a good machine for ILS landings! Nevertheless, I once committed the great sin of landing below BOAC limits. I was coming into land at Heathrow using the ILS but with Radar Controlled Landing monitoring my approach. The Britannia with the Smith Landing System was really excellent (as we used to say, it was like driving a tram downhill). I got so used to the Radar Controller saying: 'You are on the glide path; you are on the centre line,' that I just slid the Britannia on to the runway.

'Funny how the weather improved to BOAC limits just as you landed,' said the Controller. I wondered just what to say as the Controller could make an issue out of it if he liked, so I played safe and said: 'Could I thank you for your co-operation?' It proved to be a good policy because he said no more about it! The proof that I was onto a good thing came a few weeks after I went on the route as a 707 Captain. The Chief Stewardess came up to me at the end of the trip and thanked me for a good voyage and went on: 'Thank you too, Captain, for those lovely landings.' I said that surely most landings were pretty good but she told me that 'every now and then we get a terrible crumper!'

It cost around £600 per flying hour to provide in-flight training on a big jet like the 707 so it is understandable that the climax of our course, the actual flying, had to be extremely concentrated and brief. In fact, mine took exactly one week, during which I did 11 hours 30 minutes of dual. In passing, a word or two about the 707's flying characteristics may be of interest even to those who do not fly themselves. First of all the 707 was a very big, very quick aeroplane. And, especially in its 707/436 guise as purchased by BOAC, the machine had quite a high approach speed. Although this speed was normally calculated exactly for each landing, bearing in mind the weight of the aircraft, the wind, the turbulence and so on, the figure achieved and set on the 'bug', or index, on the air speed indicator was seldom less than 137 knots. This figure was, in any case, the minimum for a safe approach and like most pilots I normally added three knots or so, 'for Mum', as the saying is. So you could say that the speed on final approach was normally between 160 mph and 165 mph.

Naturally, with these pretty high speeds, the important thing was to get the machine down safely well inside the available length of the runway. And doing a peach of a landing was of quite secondary interest. The 707 was the only aeroplane I had flown where it was a complete mistake to 'play' the machine along the runway in order to ease it on to the ground at just the right altitude and speed. If you did try to do this you were liable to run out of runway in the process. Instead, the idea was to come in at the 140 knots or so you had set yourself to achieve, putting the last little bit of landing flap down, trimming the nose up a shade and then simply waiting for the monster to land itself. But there were two important things to watch. The first was that, as the engine pods were close to the ground, the wings had to be kept level the whole time, and the second was that you had to have 'cut-off-point' in mind, about fifteen per cent inside the runway threshold. If the machine had not landed by this point, and the considerable ground-cushion effect under the big low wing might stop it, then there was only one thing to do: you started pushing the stick gently forward until the wheels touched the ground.

Once you had a 707 on the ground your troubles were not over. You must first of all keep it on the ground – and they loved flying gently off again – and then you had to slow it down and stop it. This was the reason for the apparently hectic activities you might have seen in a 707 cockpit on landing. The moment the wheels touch the ground the Captain raises the lift-spoilers so the Boeing simply cannot get off again. Almost at the same moment he selects reverse thrust on the engines, and provided the First Officer calls that they have all reversed, he applies full power. And it is only after all this that he gingerly applies the brakes. This may seem very surprising to a motorist who simply puts his foot down to stop his car, even when it is travelling at 100 mph. The reason you cannot do this on an airliner is that the hydraulic disc brakes are so powerful that hard application when the machine is doing, say, 150 mph along the runway, would simply tear the tyres to shreds.

The other characteristic of the 707 which was new to most people was the way in which you took off. When this technique was developed the test pilots had two things in mind: first, how to get the monster up and away, with the minimum of noise nuisance to those near the runway; and second, how to make sure that the 'unstick' was always at a really safe speed with no risk of the machine thumping down again.

With this in mind you calculated exactly the right speed for a smooth unstick while the Captain trundled the monster along

114

the ground, getting faster and faster until the unstick speed was reached. Then with a great shout of 'Rotate' from the First Officer, the Captain gave a huge heave on the control wheel and settled the Boeing into an immediate steep-angle climb. This rather uncomfortable altitude, with the speed only 10 knots above the minimum safe climbing speed, was held until about 1,000 feet was reached. Then most of the power was taken off, to preserve the comfort of those who had, foolishly perhaps, bought houses near the airport, and the machine floated along the shallow angle, building up speed for a normal climb when the built-up area was cleared.

If all of this sounds rather a fearsome process I would only say that it was perfectly safe, performed by a fit, alert, well-trained crew. But there is still a very great deal to be said for building airports on coastal sites where approaches and climb-outs may both be made over water, and where 'noise abatement procedures' are quite unnecessary.

We learned how to deal with all these things, but the 707 also suffered from Dutch Roll. When you brought it into land it would start to roll from side to side. It was not a bad defect but it could be a bit awkward at night, when the runway lights seemed to be going from one side of the nose to the other. What you did was to use the rudder to hold the ship steady but even so, sometimes, it could produce what that Stewardess called a 'crumper'. I suppose the other feature was that the 707 had quite a high approach speed. You could calculate it but I always used 140 knots, which was quite OK except for very short runways. Which reminds me of one of my few disquieting experiences. We were flying from New York to that rather delicious holiday island of Nassau. We already knew that the longest runway was closed for maintenance and we had calculated that if we came in at 132 knots we could get in quite easily on the shorter cross runway. Imagine my worry when we came in over the last palm trees to hear the Flight Engineer say, 'Complete hydraulic failure Captain!' Luckily the 707 had a reserve hydraulic system with a limit of twelve applications of the brakes. Of course I used the normal reverse power on the engines and then did the twelve brake dabs the rules allowed. But it was a very short runway by 707 standards and we used the whole of the length available. In fact, although the wheels were still on the runway, the nose was just over the grass. By careful use of forward and reverse power on the engines we taxied to the tarmac and I was very relieved to hear the Station Engineer tell me: 'I've tightened up that hydraulic union, Captain, and filled up the tank so you won't have any more trouble.'

So it was hard to avoid trouble completely. Take engine failure. I was over Shannon Airport in Ireland and Shanwick Control cleared me to climb from the 20,000 ft I was holding up to 28,000 ft. So I put the Rolls-Royce engines up to climb power and as I did so the port outer engine's instrument all went to zero. So I reported the fact to Shanwick, that I was returning to Heathrow. They cleared me to proceed south out of the Atlantic air-routes and dump fuel down to the Heathrow landing weight. Just for your information, the 707 will fly quite well on two engines so the loss of just one engine is not a worry at all. When we got back to Heathrow, it took the engineers just five minutes to discover that the quill-shaft (an intentionally slimmed down area so there would never be any friction involved) had sheared. BOAC is a very efficient airline and had already positioned another 707 beside the point where we parked. The passengers transferred quickly to the other aircraft and off we went to New York, with the passenger baggage!

During a flight break, I was once running along a beautiful beach in Bermuda when I slipped into a hole and broke my Achilles tendon. Although you would have expected them to be more obliging, the Americans who operated the only surgical unit on the island in those days, refused to operate on my leg. And when I got home to England the surgeon who knitted my tendon together said it was a difficult operation which should have been done much sooner.

'Damn Yanks,' he said, 'they should be more helpful.' Anyway, to cut a long story short, I was off duty for four months. So I did not face my Check Captain with too much confidence.

'Bad luck, Howard,' he said, 'times are hard and we can only give you forty minutes to get used to the 707 again. And then we are off to Shannon for the check.'

'And I bet the weather at Shannon is terrible,' I volunteered.

And it certainly was. The cloud base was 250 feet and the wind was gusting across the runway at 20 knots. After the usual ILS approach I did a three-engine landing. Then we had an engine failure on the climb out and another on the approach. And finally I had to negotiate a twin-engine landing. I passed the check but I did not exactly thank the Training Department for their generosity. But the high standards which British Airways and its predecessors have always had is the reason why the British company is the world's number one international airline.

Off on the routes as a 707 skipper, the job was really much the same as it had been on the Brit, except that our greater range meant that we never had to land at Gander in Newfoundland and naturally, as we were cruising at about 570 mph, all the flight times were much shorter. The average time to New York by 707 was seven-and-a-half hours, instead of eleven-and-a-half hours which was usual on Brits. I was somewhat surprised to find that I did not feel any less tired at the end of the shorter 707 flight. And I have come to the conclusion that pilots get tired by the mile and not by the hour, as I have no doubt the managements of airlines have always hoped. I am certainly pleased that BALPA and the medical profession are looking in to the question of fatigue in pilots who operate high-speed and high-altitude machines. From seeing BOAC Captains every year at the 25 Club Party, which BOAC so generously provides for those who have done 25 years or more with the airline, I feel fairly certain that the number of flying hours per year being flown these days on 707s, VC10s and Jumbos is too high. The men just should not be showing their age so quickly.

It was not very long before I got stuck into the groove, as it were, of 707 flying with alternate trips to New York, to Chicago and to Toronto, and sometimes a drive down to the sunshine of the West Indies or South America. We had quite a big crew, ten in all and there were usually two or three other crews in town wherever we stopped. So whatever you liked to do, whether it was going to the beach, up the Hudson River, off to Niagara Falls or to the Congress at Washington, you could usually find someone who would like to go along with you.

9

BOAC Pensioner and Caledonian Pilot

Although the big American monster was certainly very reliable and my wife Joan became quite surprised at the fact that I was always home on the day she was expecting me, delays at major airports were now beginning to build up and you could certainly not often be sure of taking off on schedule. All too many of the 707 Captains of those days had just resigned themselves to the idea that a late departure always meant a late arrival into New York. But I used to take pride in getting my passengers to their destination on time, provided we had not left more than about 20 minutes late. This was really quite good fun and I had all sorts of ways of cutting off a few minutes.

First of all I used to insist on the fastest possible routing even if this sometimes meant scrapping the flight plan and doing another. Then, if one local routing out of London to the west was congested, I would switch to another, rather than accept 20 minutes or so waiting for take-off clearance. I recall the fury, one day, of Pan-American and TWA, when I declared my route to be visual to Southampton, on the air route from there to the Scilly Islands, and from there to South of Shannon Airport in Ireland. The somewhat bemused man in the control tower accepted this and gave me immediate clearance for take-off. As I taxied out past a line of jets waiting for clearance along the official route through Reading, Bristol and South

119

Wales, an American voice came through everyone's earphones: 'Say, London Airways, is this an example of giving preference to the British Airlines?'

'No, Sir,' came the reply, 'Flight 509 just hit on a good route out before you did. Do you wish to change your routing too?'

But Pan-American stuck by the book – and the official route – as they always do, and I reached New York 15 minutes before him.

Another way of making up time, I discovered, was to keep a very careful check on the wind speeds being found by the weather ships. Often a switch of a few thousand feet in operating height would get you a more favourable wind and clip quite a few minutes off the total flight time.

Then there's the obvious fact that the lower you flew, especially against the normal westerly winds, the faster you went. So I used to calculate the amount of fuel I expected to have over New York on arrival, and once this was an absolutely safe amount, I would ask for clearance down to a lower altitude. Soon I would have that satisfaction of skating past the various aircraft I could see above me.

Finally, BOAC then had a very slow descent procedure which, like every one else, I followed when I was on schedule. But when I was late I used to use the much faster cruising procedure, down to the legal limit of 25,000 feet. This again cut off quite a few minutes. Everyone to his own taste of course, and I suppose that nowadays you could not get away with my procedures, but it used to give me great pleasure to announce on the Public Address:

'Well, ladies and gentlemen, as you know there was congestion at London Airport and we left there 12 minutes late. However, I am pleased to be able to tell you that down to the left-hand side you can see the city of Boston and we shall be in New York on schedule.'

In the Autumn of 1963 someone threw a large bombshell into my fairly happy and organised life. It happened this way. BALPA, the pilots' union, wrote me a rather cryptic letter: 'If you get in touch with the Personnel Manager of BOAC,' they said, 'you will hear something to your advantage.'

120

If nothing else, this certainly made me inquisitive. But I was scarcely prepared for the rather amazing statement which this particular official made when I called at his office.

'Captain Fry, I am instructed to tell you that, owing to various negotiations between the Pilots' Association and BOAC you may, if you wish, resign from BOAC at the end of the year, and you will receive not only a cash payment in settlement of your accrued leave, but also the full pension, now, which you would have received at the normal retiring age of 55.'

My first reaction was to ask if the management had gone quietly mad. The Personnel Manager wearily agreed that he thought so too when he first heard about it. In effect, it appeared they had made a mistake. They had kindly offered premature retirement to a few Captains who had not been able to convert to jets, only to be told by the ever-vigilant union, that they were prevented by their constitution from offering better pension conditions to one group of pilots than they were providing for the remainder. Thus BOAC had been forced to allow anyone to retire on these exceptionally generous terms. A sharp trick by BALPA, if you like, but it certainly set us all quite a poser of a question:

'Should we stay on for the remaining four years, with the increasing risk, at fifty-plus, that we might fail a medical or a check flight, and get a very much reduced pension? Or should we take what was offered and go?'

To understand my dilemma I should, perhaps, explain that my salary as a 707 Captain was £5,500 and the pension I was offered for the rest of my life was £3,574 a year. Almost no one in Britain at the time got that kind of pension, and after thinking about it for some time I accepted.

So it was that after joining Imperial Airways in 1937, and having flown over 17,000 hours, I took off from London Airport on the 8th November 1963 on my last trip with Imperial's successor, BOAC. As is usual, BOAC gave me a specially nice trip, and except for the nostalgia of leaving all my old friends, I very much enjoyed it.

On the first day we nipped across the Atlantic, that I had got to know so well, in just six-and-a-half hours, and landed at Dorval, Montreal's fine modern airport. I just had one night at the old Mount Royal Hotel, a fine old place where I had spent many happy evenings, before taking off again for Los Angeles. The flight, up in the cool bump-free air, right over the United States was always a thrill; the broad expanse of the Middle West with its huge fertile farms and immense lakes; then the mighty peaks of the Rocky Mountains; the rough tough mountain country of Colorado and Utah, the scene for all those Western thrillers; then the flight in the evening across the Mojave Desert; and at last a landing through the permanent smog at Los Angeles International.

Our next stretch was from San Francisco to Honolulu so we flew up to America's most attractive city on the local Western Airlines. I was certainly grateful for a chance to see San Francisco again, with its breezy climate and breath-taking views across the Bay or out into the Pacific. Everywhere I had to say goodbye to people I had worked with for years so it all had its sad side too. Then, for the last time on 12th November I flew across the 2,500 miles of ocean to the exotic, if rather flashy, Hawaiian Islands. The weather, as always, was splendid and I was excited as usual to see the snow-capped peaks of 13,000 ft Mauna Kea and Mauna Loa as we flew past Hawaii in the evening light.

Naturally, in Honolulu I hired a car and drove out with my crew for a picnic at Hanauma Bay, where Joan and I had had many happy times. And we went to the Queen's Surf Restaurant, another of my favourites. This lovely old spot provided a wonderful blend of the Hawaiian Luau-type food – succulent pork or beef served in the open air – to the accompaniment of gentle Hawaiian guitar music and graceful Hawaiian dancing. Add the flickering light of masses of the traditional torches and the murmur of the waves lapping on the beach and you had the real feel of Honolulu.

All too soon I was heading back for San Francisco, New York and London. The Americans had a very thoughtful, kindly way of dealing with these rather sad occasions. And every Air Traffic Control Station across the States gave the same sort of friendly last message:

'Sacramento Control has been glad to work with Captain Howard Fry these past years. And we now wish you, Captain, a very happy retirement.' It didn't quite bring tears to my eyes, but it was certainly a very friendly gesture.

Finally on 17th November at 9.40 on a cold night I brought Boeing Foxtrot Metro into land at Heathrow for my very last flight in BOAC. It would be good to report that there was some friendly message from British Air Traffic Control or that someone in the BOAC flying staff management turned out to thank me for my 26 years of work. In truth nothing whatever happened, and, except for one or two members of the crew having a last quick drink with me, I was just left to disappear into the autumn night.

You could say that a pension of £3,574 for life was a good enough farewell but I still think BOAC's human relations were pretty bad in those days. And I was glad to see that in later days one of the fleet managers was usually on hand to meet skippers on their last trips, and many of them got a bit of a write up in the *BOAC News*. I am sure this sort of appreciation made those who remain feel that the often devoted work of Captains was appreciated.

I immediately had new plans: I had always wanted to try my hand at flying a helicopter and had some hopes that a retired Naval Officer friend and I might be able to start a helicopter taxi service.

Learning to fly 'choppers' with the redoubtable Polish instructor Pete Peckowski was very hard work but when I finally got my commercial licence on 'choppers' I felt a real sense of achievement. The course was at Kidlington Aerodrome, near Oxford, and included such astonishing feats as flying down below ground into a stone quarry and then issuing out again to the amazement of bystanding farm workers.

I have never been a rich man and in the ordinary way I suffer few regrets about this. But one of the few reasons why I should like to have money running out of my ears would be that I could then use a 'chopper' as my normal means of transport. I still say that, if you can afford it, there is no more astonishing means of travel. Given a decent-sized garden you can take off from your own house; once airborne you can fly happily along just above roads or railways without any need for complicated airline type navigation; and wherever you want to go, you can almost certainly find a level spot the size of a tennis court, which is all you need for landing. And, of course, chopper-owners have the remarkable privilege of being able to fly right into the centre of London, over all the traffic jams, and land in the heart of things at Battersea Heliport.

Our little plan for a helicopter taxi service depended on finding large firms in Somerset (the chosen area) who would be willing to put up most of the capital, and on discovering a suitable base from which to operate the aircraft. I tackled the second of these problems first by approaching Bath City Council. They had no expectation of ever acquiring an airport and the idea of a heliport rather attracted them. But there was a public outcry about possible noise.

This we were able to solve by flying a small helicopter into the rather underused playing field suggested by the Council, whilst the borough surveyor recorded the noise levels on a decibel meter. It is interesting to recall that the chopper was found to be quieter than a big lorry and much quieter than an express on the Western Region line close by. So approval for the use of the field was given, in principle.

In the meantime, I had been making quite good progress with the younger, air-minded directors of the two shoe firms, Clark's of Street and Morland's of Glastonbury. They came for demonstration flights and could see the huge savings of time involved in the many cross-country trips both companies had to make. Unfortunately, however, the senior directors of both concerns took a much more old-fashioned view.

'What's wrong with the company car and chauffeur?' they asked; and although the younger men tried to get them to put up the capital, in the end the scheme had to be abandoned.

A little later I had another surprise development. I was

having a drink in the White Horse, a pub near Heathrow, when I met another BOAC pensioner, who told me that Caledonian Airways were looking for Britannia Pilots. So I rang Stewart Calder, their Operations Director.

'Oh yes, Captain Fry,' he said, 'I've got you on my list. Can you come and see me tomorrow and start working for us next week?' I was a bit taken aback by his enthusiasm but I went to see him just the same. He went straight to the point.

'What do BOAC pay you not to fly for them?'

'Well that's a bit much, but since you ask, my pension is just over £3,500.'

He then said: 'Well, they pay you £3,500 not to fly for them and I'll pay you £3,500 to fly for us.' That gave me an income of £7,000 a year, quite a lot of money in those days, 1965. So I started life in the private enterprise section of civil flying.

He wanted me to start flying the next week, but we could not arrange it quite as soon as that. So a couple of days later I was fixing details with Stu, a pleasantly informal character. And on 9th March 1965 I found myself once again at the controls of a BOAC Britannia, Victor King, on a flight from London to Shannon Airport in Ireland. Also on board was my old 707 colleague, Ronnie Stone, and supervising the operation was BOAC Training Captain Lovelace.

It was a strange sensation for Ronnie and I to go back, as it were, five years in time, in order to renew our acquaintance with the old Britannia. But it is a simple aeroplane and it took us only a couple of flights to get our hands in again, plus, of course, a short spell on the Britannia simulator at Cranebank.

Once this was done and our licences were suitably endorsed, Ronnie and I found ourselves once again airline pilots. But this time we were paid twice. I do not know what arrangements Ronnie Stone made but I used to tell my friends the truth – that I really had two employers:

'Caledonian Airways pay me £3,500 a year to fly their Britannias – and BOAC pay me another £3,500 not to fly their 707s.'

It was a splendid arrangement.

After 26 years in BOAC, an independent airline like Caledonian came as quite a shock. I am not suggesting that either the flying standards or the maintenance were poor. In fact, both were pretty good. But there was a refreshing lack of frills and formality about our 'wee Scots airline' as we called it.

To begin with, the ground staff was extremely small in number and everyone just had to pull his weight. Then there were just enough offices, and office chairs, to go round. And to save expense, the pilots and the engineers and stewardesses did much of the ground work themselves. Here are some examples:

Shepherding of passengers: whereas BOAC employed masses of traffic girls, Caledonian expected their steward-esses to get the passengers on and off the aircraft.

Flight Planning: instead of BOAC's big establishment of operations staff, Caledonian employed a couple of people to lay down the principles. Captains and co-pilots were expected to do their own flight plans and obtain their own ATC clearances.

Loading the fuel: instead of BOAC's staff of ground engineers, Caledonian used the flight engineers to load the fuel on their aircraft.

And these economies actually meant the Caledonian staff were far from sullen and unenthusiastic. As everyone thought he, or she, was doing a really full job they were happier than if they had been underemployed. In any case you could not really complain that you had to work hard in an airline where the Chairman sometimes exchanged his office chair for a pilot's seat and flew one of his own aircraft around the world. In 1965, Adam Thomson, Caledonian's very able but also very democratic boss, still kept his hand in as a DC7C Captain.

My first job in Callie, as we always called it, was to 'fly the Haj'.

This not very pleasant form of flying consisted of loading as many Muslims as you could possibly get into an airliner and then flying them from their homeland to Jeddah, in Saudi Arabia. Here they continued to Mecca, the Holy City of their faith, by bus. Once they had completed the Haj, or pilgrimage to Mecca, they were entitled to call themselves Hajjis and if they were men, they could dye their beards ginger.

Only too often, unfortunately, the pilgrims did not maintain at all the standards of attitude that you get with most airline passengers. But although the pilots and the cabin crew did not exactly enjoy the Haj, it was recognised in the independent airlines as an essential way of making some solid cash before the season of package tours and Atlantic charters started.

In Caledonian's case they had the contract for the Moroccan Haj and really this was quite painless. We stayed at a reasonable family hotel in Rabat where the rooms and meals, although not up to BOAC standard, were certainly quite adequate.

The flight to Jeddah with 130 pilgrims on board took about eight-and-a-half hours whilst with the plane empty we were able to fly back in about nine-and-a-half against the prevailing westerlies. Caledonian's careful flight operations people back at Gatwick had estimated that it would quite often be necessary for us to land at Benghazi to refuel. But, having flown the Brit for years and discovered ways of getting the best possible speed and range, I was able to prove to the management that intermediate landings were never needed. Whereas BOAC might have been cross and even pompous about it, the Caledonian bosses were only too pleased to find they were wrong, and they could, in fact, save time and money by flying direct.

The whole object of the Haj was to make money quickly, so all we ever had was one or two days off in between the fairly long flights and naturally the pilgrims could not stay in Saudi Arabia forever, so for every Haj there has to be a return-Haj. This took place every year in April and was a repeat of the previous performance, except that it was the heavily loaded return flights from Jeddah that needed the most careful attention if an intermediate landing was to be avoided. But again, with I think one exception, we managed all of them non-stop, although it often took over ten hours of bumping along the North African coast. Other pilots may be interested in what we found was the best way of getting 130 pilgrims direct from Jeddah to Rabat against the headwinds.

First of all, we had to be very ruthless about the baggage and see it was not overweight. Then we used to try to get away during the night or in the very early morning in order to get the lowest temperature and the best fuel load. Once off, the scheme was to keep quite low – even down to 8,500 feet – where there was sometimes a tail-wind and seldom a strong headwind. This not only enabled us to cover a lot of ground quickly but it also burnt off quite a lot of heavy fuel. Then you had to judge the right moment to climb right up to about 24,000 feet, where although the headwind would be high the fuel consumption would be low. And from then on to Rabat the idea was to keep climbing, as the weight of the aircraft reduced, so that the consumption would come down still further. I often got up to around 30,000 ft on the last stages of the flight and this certainly provided an encouraging range in case a diversion should ever have been needed.

The Haj was also a way for Caledonian Airways to try out their Britannias and see what they could do with them. As soon as the Haj flights were over we put the Britannias on the flights they had been bought for – the Atlantic services. Caledonian had lists of all the Scottish clubs and societies in USA and Canada. And they were very efficient in sending marketing people to call on them to persuade them to use a Scottish airline. The upshot of it was that Caledonian actually carried more people across the Atlantic than BOAC in their first season of Brit operation. As an old BOAC man, I must remind you that all the Callie flights were full of charter passengers, whereas the BOAC flights were usually only three-quarters full. And, of course, the Callie fares were somewhat lower. But perhaps Callie were lucky in that Scottish people are rather patriotic and rather like to fly on a plane with the Scottish lion displayed boldly on the tail.

The flying programme in Caledonian was a fantastic contrast with my rather stereotyped life in BOAC. Instead of set routes, for each of which you received careful route training, in Caledonian you flew anywhere in the world with just a written briefing before you left. For example, in my first month of ordinary (non-Haj) flying with Callie, I flew to Munich, Istanbul, Dubrovnik and Ljubljana. In the following month I flew to Leopoldville, Malta, Athens, Palma, Ibiza, Toronto and New York. And all with just a page or two in a folder called the Captain's brief.

It was all quite an education, in what you can do if you try, but it did require careful study of the complicated network of European air-routes, some of which were not very familiar to me. And it did mean that I had to study the let-down procedures for the new airports and follow them with great accuracy. I must say that, once I got settled in to the Caledonian way of doing things, I was inclined to think that perhaps BOAC overdid the regulations, the checking and the spoonfeeding.

In those days, as a Callie Captain, you were more or less a self-contained unit. You left England with a Captain's float, usually consisting of dollar travellers cheques, which might amount to around £1,000. This was used to pay for landing fees, hotel accommodation, for crew transport and the cash allowances to the crew. Naturally, everything had to be properly accounted for and making up the accounts at the end of a trip was quite a chore.

On the other hand, Callie were quite generous and there was a pleasant informality about the way they did things. My interview with Stu Calder before I did my first flight to New York for Callie illustrates this:

'Morning, Stu,' I said, 'what was it you wanted to see me about?'

'Just wanted to put you in the picture, Howard, on the way we do things.'

'Go ahead.'

'The first thing is this. No doubt, as it's so cheap, you'll want to buy yourself a half of Scotch from the bar?'

'Yes, I should think so.'

'Well, let me give you a bit of advice. I'd buy two half bottles if I were you.'

'What do I want the second one for?'

'I'm coming to that. When you get to the hotel in New York, don't embarrass the room clerk by saying anything about it, but just gently slide the half bottle around the screen on her counter.'

'That would be pretty generous of me.'

'Well, that's true, but you'll be surprised to find that when you get to your room, you've got a very nice little suite of lounge, bedroom and bathroom.'

'Good Heavens!'

'Yes, it always works and it's nice to have a bit of room, especially if you're going to throw a party.'

'I didn't know I was throwing a party.'

'Well, the crew expect it and it's very good for morale. But don't worry about the cost. After all the hard stuff doesn't cost much from the bar on the aircraft and you can charge all the mixers and the beer on the Captain's account book.'

'I can, can I?'

'Certainly. But I always write it down as light refreshments on arrival. And no one ever argues.'

So off I went on my first Callie trip to New York. The same careful operations man who had assured me I would have to land at Benghazi between Jeddah and Rabat also had me scheduled to make a call at Gander between Gatwick and New York. Once again he was underestimating the performance of the Brit and we made it non-stop quite comfortably in 11 hours 25 minutes. The secret was to flight-plan first of all for Gander; then approaching Gander to replan for New York, with Philadelphia as alternate. By this time you were usually so high that the fuel needed was very small and there was quite a slice of reserve fuel for waiting about in the stack as well.

Thus began three years of rather exciting and refreshing

130

flying. It was a kind of an Indian Summer of aviation for me. Callie flying just seemed like flying for the enjoyment of it and I always had the feeling that I was helping a small airline to get bigger: rather a good feeling.

Caledonian, incidentally, did quite a bit of trooping and that certainly introduced me to some new parts of the world. One of them was Bardufoss in the mountain snows of Norway. To say Bardufoss was a tricky place to fly to would be a massive understatement. It is the only place in the world, so far as I know, where the Instrument Landing System ended in a pile of stones on a deserted hillside, and one of the few places where the runway was enclosed with hills in virtually every direction. There was only one way in. You followed the various radio beacons up the coast and into the nearest fjord to Bardufoss. By this time you began to receive signals from the Bardufoss ILS, and soon you could establish yourself on the beam and on the glide path way out from the field. To make doubly sure in these rugged mountains you tuned in the beacons as well as the ILS and flew the beam with meticulous care. At 400 ft came the moment of decision. You either turned left about 40 degrees and saw the runway ahead of you or you climbed out, as fast as you could back to the beacon and out to sea. On landing, the place was very beautiful with pines and firs in all directions and an airport restaurant made from massive cut logs.

Meanwhile, Caledonian had signed a contract to take part in an oil lift from Tanzania to Zambia and I was posted forthwith to Dar es Salaam.

Flying from there to Lusaka and Ndola in Zambia brought back memories of flying in and out of the harbour on flying boats. I could not help contrasting the beauty and breezy coolness of the old flying boat base, right in the centre of the town, to the dusty heat and remote position of the new land aerodrome. As usual, it seemed absurd to me that, with so many of the important cities of the world sited close to stretches of water, we had given up flying boats with so little real consideration of their merits.

Using Britannia aircraft to fly diesel oil (our particular

cargo) into Zambia was not, technically, a very bright operation. We used more fuel in order to make the return flight than
we were able to deliver. But, at any rate, at the start of the
operation, Zambia was genuinely short of fuel and had no
means of bringing it in by road. But as more road tankers
arrived and the road itself was improved, our flights became
less and less necessary. And I suspect they were continued
largely in order to show public solidarity with Zambia.

It was about this time that, although Britain had broken off
relations with Rhodesia, the capital, Salisbury, was still the Air
Traffic Control Centre responsible for most of our route. It
was amusing to note the courtesy and efficiency Salisbury
ATC displayed. As soon as I flew into their area, often after
having great difficulty in maintaining communications with
Nairobi, who controlled the northern part of the route, up
would come the loud clear voice of Salisbury.

'Good morning, November Zulu, this is Salisbury. You are
clear to proceed through our area to land at Ndola. Here is the
Ndola weather...' and the clipped South African voice would
give us the latest weather at Lusaka, Ndola and Salisbury. If,
as often happened, the Salisbury weather was much the best,
the voice would go on, 'If you wish to divert to Salisbury you
can be sure of a friendly welcome.' Naturally we never availed
ourselves of Salisbury's invitation.

Various things stick in my mind from my Caledonian days.
One was when my crew and I had three rather prized days in
New York. Out of the blue the Callie manager asked us
whether we would fly down to Georgetown in Guyana and
take the last of the British garrison home to their base in
Belfast. I'm pleased to say that all my boys and girls were
happy to oblige the airline. 'Tommy's been good to us so we'll
be good to Tommy,' were words they used and I'll explain
that. Tommy was Captain Adam Thompson, the Callie Chairman, and he had just taken a Callie crew to the Waldorf
Astoria, the best hotel in New York. Anyway, off we went to
Georgetown, where I was surprised to find a man I knew quite
well from my BOAC days.

'I don't think I'll take any notice of this,' I told him,

132

referring to the flight plan. 'I'll leave at five and go straight to Santa Maria.' He looked at me in a mood of shock and horror.

'You can't do that,' he gasped.

I put my hand up to my Caledonian cap and told him, 'I work for Callie now, not BOAC, and they like their Captains to save time and money for them.' I explained that the wind changed to one straight down the runway in the evening and that if I flew at 22,000 feet, instead of the 18,000 they suggested, I should get a much better wind. So indeed I did take-off at 5pm and I did fly direct to Santa Maria. And far from getting the rebuke the ground staff expected, I had a letter from Adam Thompson thanking me for using my initiative and telling me that I had saved the airline £1,000. Another surprise I recall was when we had landed a Britannia at Detroit and had then taken two cars to drive to New York for our next service. We spent the night at Niagara Falls and were amazed to get a phone call from the New York manager. How he knew we were there I don't know but he asked us to go to Ottawa, pick up a Brit and fly it with a full load of Burns Society passengers to London. Again we were pleased to help but it was still quite extraordinary that the airline had found us.

I could understand that Caledonian Airlines decided to give up Britannias and go in for Boeing 707s. But I met Adam Thompson and discussed it with him. He was able to give me some interesting figures.

'At Gatwick,' he said, 'we are thirteen miles from the Vickers Factory and five thousand miles from Boeing at Seattle. Yet Boeing replied to our letter first and they sent their team to see us first. Furthermore, the Boeing team were really experienced pilots and engineers and Vickers sent marketing men with nice Oxford accents, so really, I had no choice but to buy Boeing.'

I am not sure he was right but you can see his point of view. And you can understand why America had beaten Britain in the world of airliner building.

I was quite pleased, personally, when Caledonian started to take delivery of 707s. As a 707 Captain in BOAC I thought I would be able to transfer from Britannias to 707s. Unfor tunately, the Air Registration Board who control these things decided that there were too many differences between the BOAC 707s and the newer versions bought by Caledonian. And they refused to accept my 707 licence unless I did another course. So, understandably, I had to retire from Caledonian. You could not possibly have expected Callie to pay for a new course for someone who only had a year or so to go before stopping flying entirely. And to be fair about it I had had a good innings since I had joined the Air Force in 1932 – 35 years and 18,806 flying hours ago. Perhaps I was right to call my talks to the Rotarians and the Women's Institutes, 'The Best Years of Flying'.

EPILOGUE

One of the drawbacks of being an Airline pilot is that you have to stop flying at around 60. When I had to cease flying for Caledonian we simply decided to pack it all in and retire to Cornwall where Joanie's parents came from.

Unfortunately, I met a lot of Cornish businessmen who tried hard to get me to run a Cornwall to London air service. Frankly, this was not a very good idea because the London Airports Authorities were not keen on another air service which would occupy air space but would only bring in a few passengers. They made the condition that we would only be welcomed if we ran an inter-airport shuttle as well.

After a great deal of discussion between the Cornish businessmen and a group of flying people who had now joined me, it was decided that we form a little company called Westward Airways and fly both a shuttle between Heathrow and Gatwick and a West Country service. Unfortunately, the Cornish business firms did not invest the large sums we expected, so we started our little Airline with two leased Britten Norman airliners, and rather less capital than we would really have liked.

Westward Airways made quite a good start with our various jobs but the trade unions adopted the very awkward attitude we could have expected in those days. Although we flew the flight between the two airports in only 18 minutes against an hour by taxi, we did not make a good profit. This was because the unions told the airport staff that they were not to provide any information about our service or any instructions about how to board our aircraft. Even more damaging was the union instruction that union members were not to refuel our aircraft at Heathrow. This, of course, involved the expense and delay of refuelling at Bournemouth.

The West Country service gave us fewer problems and you could say it was a remarkable success. We provided a good businessman's service from Newquay and Plymouth to Gatwick as well as a day return service to the little St Mary's Airport in Scilly. To get the most out of our two little Islanders we also carried a full load of lobsters and crayfish to Quimper in France, whenever our agents had arranged it. This was rather a good period in my life. The Islander was rather a nice little aircraft and I enjoyed flying it. Surprised? Well, although I had flown big four-engined planes all my life there is something rather sedate about them and it was rather fun to fly something a bit more nimble. And we had a great deal of satisfaction in getting from Heathrow to Gatwick in something amazingly short like 18 minutes. Here it would be good to record that Air Traffic Control were really helpful and obliging. Perhaps because I was the most experienced of our pilots, I flew quite a number of these shuttles between the airports and really they were great fun with some of them taking as little as 15 minutes. Air Traffic Control observed us on their radar and they would often slip us in just after a landing aircraft.

Everything in life can be improved and after operating for a year we people in Westward Airways decided on various minor improvements in our services. For example, we changed the operating times of the shuttle and we decided to run more services from Plymouth. Unfortunately, before these could be tried out, we had our first piece of really bad luck. One of our least experienced pilots ran off the end of the runway at Scilly and came to rest in a daffodil field. It all sounds rather funny but it involved us having to borrow some more money from our merchant bankers. After a lot of discussion it was decided that we needed £25,000. All the directors agreed to do their best to raise this sum. It is a shame to have to report that, though I managed to get additional investment of £20,000 from businessmen, the other directors raised nothing at all and our merchant bankers called the receivers in. A sad end for a promising little enterprise? Certainly, but it is good news for the West Country service that it is now run by an associate of British Airways. As for the shuttle between Heathrow and Gatwick it is not needed now because the coach service on the M25 is just about adequate, even if it is a bit slower than we all hoped.

So that was the end of my flying career, a career that spanned nearly 40 years, starting with the 75 mph bi-plane Avro 504 and culminating in the 580 mph Boeing 707. And you can say that I spent more than two years of my life actually in the sky – in 28 different sorts of aircraft – and mostly that I have enjoyed every moment!

know
the
game

Rowing

by Roger Vincett

Published in collaboration with the Amateur Rowing Association

CONTENTS

INTRODUCTION

This book has been written to interest you in rowing and further your understanding of the sport. It is, after all, one of the oldest sports in the world, going back thousands of years to the time of ancient Greece. In its modern form the sport first developed in England in the eighteenth century, when the professional watermen of the time frequently challenged each other to rowing matches. In 1715 Thomas Doggett started a sculling race for young watermen on the River Thames and this annual race for the Doggett's Coat and Badge is now the oldest existing rowing or sculling race in the world. The first University Boat race between Oxford and Cambridge took place in 1829, and Henley Royal Regatta dates back to 1839.

The popularity of rowing has steadily increased throughout the world in modern times and now over 50 countries belong to the International Rowing Federation. Our own Amateur Rowing Association includes about 470 clubs, universities, colleges and schools with a total membership of over 26,000 members—men, women, boys and girls. Once rowing was a sport for the professionals and the leisured upper classes, but now it can be enjoyed by anyone living near water, whether on a lake, canal, river or even the sea.

It is hoped that this book will provide a stimulus to those who have never tried rowing, and a reinforcement of basic ideas to those who are already involved in it. Whatever your level of knowledge and experience of rowing it is worth mentioning that it is the team sport above all others. Through its complete unison of effort and movement rowing in a crew builds a great spirit of togetherness, and whether you choose the crew or the single sculling boat you will find that rowing can offer you enjoyment and competition second to none.

TYPES OF RACING BOAT

There are two categories of racing boat used in rowing, the ROWING BOAT for 8, 4 or 2 persons, and the SCULLING BOAT for 1, 2, or 4 scullers.

In rowing you hold one oar with two hands, a sculler holds a scull in each hand. Therefore a scull is correspondingly shorter and lighter than an oar, with a smaller blade area.

Over the years racing boats, known as shells, have become long and slender, and through modern methods of construction, such as cold moulding, have become very thin and light. They are also very expensive and require careful handling. The smaller boats are very difficult to balance and therefore the greater is the skill needed to row them properly. They are made from thin ply-wood built round a frame of ribs. Recent experiments have produced fibre-glass and plastic boats. There are no restrictions to the dimensions of a boat, although at the novice stage of rowing you are likely to use more stable craft. Such boats are wider, flatter and heavier than shell boats, and are easier for beginners to handle.

Eights

The racing eight at full speed is one of the most exciting sights in rowing. The boat is some 56 ft. long or over but only 24 inches wide at its widest point. Its weight is between 200 and 250 lbs. and it is capable of reaching speeds of 18 ft. per second, and it is always steered by a coxswain.

The Eight

Fours

Racing fours can be with or without a coxswain. They are between 40 and 42 ft. in length. Coxswainless boats are steered by one of the crew, who has one foot in a pivoting shoe to which the rudder lines are attached.

The coxed four

The coxless four

Pairs

Pairs can also be with or without a coxswain. The coxed pair is the slowest of all rowing boats and you will often see the coxswain steering from the front of the boat in a lying down position. All other coxed boats are usually steered from the stern. Pairs are about 32 ft. long.

Single Sculling Boats

This is often a 'tailor made' boat built to suit the individual sculler. Therefore its weight can be as low as 30 lbs. Its length is about 26 ft.

Double Sculling Boats

These are for two scullers sitting one behind the other. Many coxswainless pairs are convertible into double sculling boats. Its length is approximately the same as the coxless pair.

Quadruple Sculling Boats

These have only recently appeared in top class men's racing, although they have been long established in women's racing, where they are used with a coxswain. In men's racing they are coxless and are the second fastest of all racing boats. Again, the quadruple sculling boat can be converted from a four, although it is not as successful as the purpose-built boat.

The coxed pair

The coxless pair

The single scull

The double scull

The quadruple scull

5

PARTS OF THE BOAT

All racing boats are fitted with riggers, sliding seats and stretchers. These are integral parts of the boat, all designed to make the rowing stroke as mechanically efficient as possible, and as such they must be kept in good running order.

Riggers

This is the usual term given to the metal stays which protrude from the side of the boat. At present the most common types of rigger have either two or three stays. Two-stay riggers, especially of aerofoil design, are much better in terms of reducing wind resistance and cutting through washes. Three-stay riggers, because they are attached to the boat in three places, spread the load more evenly, and therefore there is less strain on the boat. Either type is preferable to the traditional five-stay riggers.

At the point where the rigger stays meet is located the rowing SWIVEL. This is a moving rowlock, often called a GATE, which pivots freely round a vertical THOLE PIN. This swivel supports the oar.

Modern riggers can be made to adjust so that the pin can be moved in or out, backwards or forwards, and the height of the swivel can be varied. These adjustments are necessary in providing the most comfort and the most efficiency for rowing of each individual so that you can get the best return for the effort you put into rowing each stroke.

The swivel or gate, rigger and saxboard

Saxboard

This is the reinforced top section of the side of the boat. It is through this saxboard that the riggers are bolted on to strong shoulders, which help to make up the frame of the racing boat.

Slide

The slide, together with its seat, is where you sit and move up and down the boat during the rowing stroke. It consists of two parallel runners on which the seat travels and has a stop at its front and back ends to prevent the seat sliding right off. Usually it is advisable to have the runners as long as possible (between 28 and 32 inches) so that you can use the full length of your legs during the stroke. It is not necessary for all members of a crew to slide the same distance and it is unlikely that they would, because of different lengths of leg and flexibility in the ankles.

The slide and seat

Stretcher

While you sit on your seat and travel up and down the slide, your feet are fixed by a stretcher. This consists of two inclined footrests mounted on a frame attached at the top to the inside of the saxboard, and at the bottom to the keel of the boat. The whole stretcher is movable backwards and forwards so that people of different leg lengths can be comfortably adjusted to use as much slide as possible. Once you have made this adjustment the stretcher is fixed with thumbscrews.

Your feet are held on the footrests by a leather shoe known as a CLOG, or in some practice boats, a strap. In boats fitted with long slides (over 30 inches) you very often find flexible shoes instead of clogs. These allow your heels to rise as you slide forward so that you reach a comfortable position at the front stop. The stretcher is normally angled at about 40 degrees and should be in a position where the balls of your feet are approximately in line with your seat. Again modern boats often have stretchers which can be adjusted for angle and height of the feet.

The stretcher   *Feet fixed in clogs*

Rudder

All boats have rudders except the single and double sculling boats. Rudders can be either fixed to a pin on the very stern of the boat or under the hull of the boat between the coxswain's seat and the stern. Those located under the hull are known as FIN RUDDERS and can be either attached to the fin of the boat itself or separate. The fin on a boat acts in providing some stability, and the advantage of a fin rudder is that it requires only a small movement to alter the direction of the boat. A stern rudder requires more violent application and therefore may produce a braking effect on the boat. The smaller the boat the more unsettling is the effect of the rudder on the balance of the boat, so a fin rudder is kept as small as possible. In coxed boats the coxswain steers by means of rudder lines attached through a pulley system to the rudder.

Separate fin rudder

Bow and Stern

The very necessary streamlined effect of a racing boat is completed by the narrow bow and stern which taper away almost to a point. Both these parts of the boat are usually covered in a thin material called the CANVAS, but some are covered with very thin wood. On the bow of all racing boats you should always see a small white ball called a BOBBLE. No boat is allowed to race without one of these.

Bowside

The left hand side of the boat as you face the stern. ('Starboard' in nautical terms.)

Strokeside

The right hand side of the boat as you face the stern. ('Port' in nautical terms.)

Stern rudder

Fin rudder attached to fin

The bow with regulation bobble

The Bowside and Strokeside oarsmen in a pair

8

OARS

The oar is the lever through which you produce the necessary power to make you and your boat go forward. The speed of the boat will depend upon the speed of the oar handle and the distance it moves when the blade is in the water. Oars are long, varying in length between 12 ft. and 12 ft. 8 inches, but because they are hollow they can weigh as little as 6 lbs. They have to be reinforced down the back of the shaft to give them stiffness or else they will break when you row. Sculls are lighter and shorter, measuring between 9 ft. 6 inches and 10 ft. The oar consists of 4 parts:

The oar in relation to the boat (But see p. 18 for hand positions)

1. The Handle

is a shaved-down part of the oar about 15 inches long. It is left unvarnished to provide your hands with sufficient grip. A scull handle is usually fitted with a rubber grip.

2. The Button

is a collar round the shaft of the oar to prevent it from slipping out of the gate. It is usually made of plastic and can be adjusted up and down the oar over a plastic sheath. This adjustment is made to make the leverage of the oar easier or harder. The distance between the far end of the handle and face of the button touching the gate is called the INBOARD of the oar. The remaining length of the oar right out to the tip of the blade is called the OUT-BOARD.

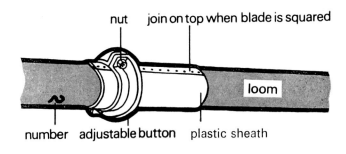

3. The Loom

is the long reinforced shaft of the oar. It is varnished and has a number on it. This number represents the position in the boat where it is to be used.

4. The Blade

The area and shape of the blade are very important. Until the late 1950s blades were long and thin, measuring about 32 inches by 6½ inches at their tip. They became known as 'needles'. But in the 1960s successful West German crews introduced a shorter, wider type of design called a 'spade' blade. While the principle of rowing is to lever the boat past the blade, the blade is in fact never anchored at one spot in the water. This is because it slips as pressure is exerted. The idea behind 'spade' blades, therefore, is to cut down this slipping by making the blade shorter and wider.

So the wider the blade, the easier it is to get a firm hold on the water, but at the same time it will feel heavier.

The type of blade which is most often used is a combination of the 'needle' and 'spade' blade. It is called a 'Mâcon' blade, so called because it was used successfully in the European championships held at Mâcon in 1959. Measuring 24 inches long and being wider than the 'needle' blade it produces a firm grip in the water, and because it is longer and less wide than the 'spade' blade it is more easily handled.

One last point about a blade is that it is curved to form a cup in the water. The more it is curved the better should be the beginning of the stroke, but if it is curved too much you will find it difficult to handle at the other end of the stroke.

When you row you must make sure that only the blade area is covered in the water. If you dig your blade too deeply so that water runs up the loom you will be slowing your boat down. This is because when you make a stroke your blade will be moving towards the stern of the boat, but your loom will be moving forward. Therefore there is a point within the blade known as a turning-point, and any water in contact with your oar inboard of that turning-point will tend to drag the boat backward.

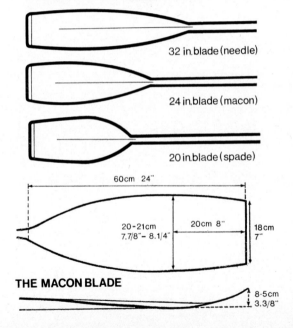

Blade Types

32 in. blade (needle)

24 in. blade (macon)

20 in. blade (spade)

60cm 24"

20-21cm
7.7/8"- 8.1/4"

20cm 8"

18cm
7"

THE MACON BLADE

8·5cm
3.3/8"

SAFETY

You must be able to swim. Unlike sailing and canoeing you cannot row very well in a life jacket. You must therefore be able to look after yourself if you fall out of the boat or if the boat capsizes or sinks. You are strongly advised to pass the Amateur Swimming Association's Bronze Level Award for Personal Survival, for unless you can swim well your rowing progress could be very slow. You should never go out in a boat unless you can swim.

If you fall out of your boat you must try to hang on to it. It is very unlikely to sink and will therefore keep you afloat. It is also a very expensive piece of equipment which is difficult to replace, and unless you keep hold of it it could turn out to be a very dangerous floating hazard for other crews or scullers on that part of the water. If no help is immediately available you should try to propel yourself and your boat towards the river bank, swimming with the direction of the current. If the boat is undamaged, you can empty the water out and continue rowing to keep warm. If you cannot row in it either wait for help, or if you are very cold run back to the boathouse for help, having made sure your boat and oars are safe.

You must also know your local water. In most rowing clubs there is usually a map of the water, and you should study this carefully. Make sure you know which way the current or tide is running, where the sharp bends are, if there are any bridges or other obstacles such as buoys or moored boats. There may also be locks, weirs, shallow or turbulent water. You must also know the local rules regarding which side of the river you row upstream and downstream.

WELCOME TO THE CLUB —
WE DON'T WANT TO LOSE YOU

SO MAKE SURE THAT YOU ARE A STRONG SWIMMER

IF YOU FALL OVERBOARD HANG ON TO THE BOAT — IT WON'T SINK

AND KNOW YOUR COURSE BEFORE STARTING OFF

Barry Appleby

CLOTHING

Whether you are rowing in the summer or the winter makes a difference to what you wear. In warm weather you will want to wear only a singlet and shorts, but when it is cold you should wear more than you think you need —you can always take things off when you get hot.

When you are learning to row a sports shirt and shorts might be your basic clothing worn under a tracksuit. If you row in competition you will wear your club singlet. But always have enough clothing to keep warm before and after a race. Rowing shorts often have a reinforced seat and therefore last longer than thin cotton ones, but it is becoming more usual to see people rowing in thicker and more comfortable woollen shorts.

You will also need a thick pair of socks to wear in the boat. These will stop blisters forming on your heels as they rub up and down in the clogs of your stretcher. Many people sew leather patches on the heels of their socks to prevent blisters. In older boats which may not have clogs at all but simply straps you will need a strong pair of old shoes.

You will certainly need something on your feet anyway when you carry the boat to and from the boathouse. Gym shoes are usually very suitable when there is a proper landing-stage, but on tidal rivers where the water level rises and falls it is better to wear Wellington boots so that you do not get your feet wet when you put the boat on to the water. Wet feet often become cold or blistered.

The most important thing is warmth and you must particularly look after your back. As you are in fact sitting down and travelling backwards in the boat make quite certain that the clothes you wear are big enough to tuck into your shorts or your track suit trousers so that the lower part of your back is well protected from the cold.

Winter Oarsman

Summer oarsman

CARRYING THE BOAT AND PUTTING IT AFLOAT

There must be some method of basic boat drill to get the boat off the rack in the boathouse and into the water. Any lack of discipline could prove very expensive. Usually the boat is stored upside down on the rack, and as a rule each member of the crew stands opposite his own rigger. On the order 'HANDS ON . . . READY . . . LIFT' given by the coxswain, the boat is gently lifted off the rack with special care to clear the riggers of any nearby boats, and carried with both hands grasping the

saxboard down to the landing stage. Always avoid holding the boat by its riggers as they could easily be strained.

It should arrive at the water's edge with its bow facing upstream, or in the case of a tidal river, facing the direction of the current. If the boat has been stored on a high rack in the boathouse it can be either carried out at shoulder height or lowered from shoulder height to waist height. Where there is only a limited space between sets of racks in the boathouse, the boat will have to be carried out on the half turn (with riggers vertical) or else you will knock all the riggers.

Once at the water's edge the boat must be turned over and set in the water. There are two ways of doing this.

(i) The boat is turned its proper way up and held by the members of the crew on one side of the boat while those on the other side crawl underneath. With everyone then on the same side of the boat it is walked out to the water and placed level in it.

(ii) The boat is lifted, or 'thrown' above the heads of the crew so that those on the water-side of the boat go underneath it. It is then lowered and placed gently in the water. See illustrations, page 14.

The procedure for lifting the boat out of the water and putting it back into the boathouse is the reverse of putting it afloat except that the boat will have to be dried with a chamois leather before it goes up on to its rack again.

Be very careful when you put a boat into the water or take it out, and make certain that it never touches the shore or the river bed. Any contact could be disastrous for a shell boat, and so with shallow water you will have to walk the boat out until it is deep enough for the boat and the crew in it to float without any danger of going aground. You must also keep a sharp look out for any underwater obstructions which could damage your boat.

1. Arriving at the water's edge

3. The boat is lowered

2. Throwing the boat

4. And set gently in the water

LEARNING YOUR ROWING

There are many opinions on the best way to teach rowing and you are quite likely to receive a lot of advice, sometimes confusing, when you are learning. But one thing you must never forget during the first stages of learning to row is that the boat goes forward as a result of the power you apply on the oar. It is therefore most important that you learn how to use the oar properly to give you the best results from the amount of effort you put into rowing each stroke.

The way you are taught to do this will vary from coach to coach, but will lie between the two extremes of coaching. One is the formal coaching of body positions, and the other is the more informal sculling method where you teach yourself to propel the boat. In fact the way you learn to row will be a combination of these two methods.

One of the most important aspects of learning to row, and one which is often overlooked, is that you must learn how to teach yourself. Your coach can only go so far, and then it is up to you. Only then will it be possible to progress a long way. It is more difficult to do if you are being coached through the body position method, but if you can develop a basic understanding of boat propulsion by improving the action of your blade both in and out of the water you will find that your improvement will be a natural progression. Even at an early stage you must try to be critical of your own rowing and that of others. You will be much encouraged by the fact that oarsmen more experienced than you are not perfect.

Every sport needs practice if you are going to be good at it, and while you might find rowing strange at first, you will soon learn the basic ideas. If you stick at it you will discover the real enjoyment of rowing in a fast-moving boat.

FIRST STEPS

Unless your coach wants you to learn your rowing in the sculling boat it is quite likely that you will start in either an indoor rowing-tank or a bank-tub fixed to the river bank. If these are not available you should start in a tub-pair or tub-four. This should be quickly followed by a proper racing boat. The speed at which you progress will depend not only on your ability and how much equipment there is available but also on the type of water on which you will be learning your rowing. For instance, a higher level of competence is needed on a fast-flowing river or tidal water than on still water.

The Bank Tub

The Tub pair

To begin with you will have to know how to get into and out of the boat without damaging it or turning it over. Have a look at the way the person in the illustrations is getting into the boat. Someone should hold the boat level for you as you step on to the centre of the front of the slide. With both hands holding the sides of the boat you should gently lower yourself on to the seat and put your feet into the clogs or straps.

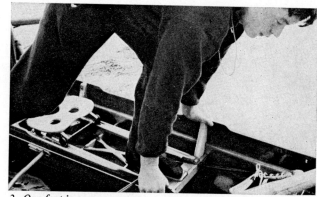

2. One foot in

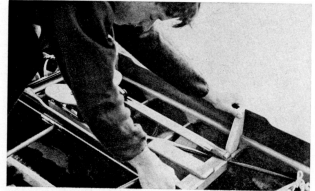

1. Hands across

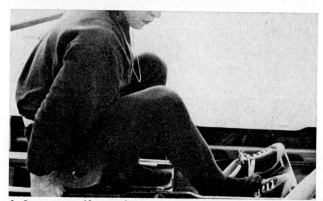

3. Lower yourself on to the seat

You should learn how to put your oar into the gate and remove it and how to adjust the position of the stretcher so that your legs are straight when your seat

Undo the gate and put the neck of the oar in

Slide the oar out and do up the gate

is as far back as possible. This is done by undoing the thumbscrews holding the stretcher in place and then moving it backward or forward. When you slide forward your shins should be as vertical as possible at the front-stop.

Straight legs at backstops

Vertical shins at front stops

You will notice that as you sit in the boat and hold the oar with its blade vertical and resting in the water, only the blade itself will be covered. This is its natural height in the water, and when you row you must see that no more than the blade is covered. You should also notice that the blade is slightly pitched forward. This will help you keep the blade covered as you row. If it is not pitched forward your blade will tend to dive below the surface of the water when you try to take a stroke.

You must also make sure that when the boat is kept level and you hold the oar handle against the lower part of your ribs (the finish of the stroke) again with the blade kept vertical, you have enough room to drop the oar handle down towards your thighs so that the blade comes clear of the water.

Holding the oar (N.B. Outside wrist should not be dropped.)

The vertical position of the blade is known as a squared blade and the first strokes you do should be with your seat fixed at the backstop and the blade kept squared all the time. This will let you feel how the blade is drawn through the water. The line the blade follows should be a continuous oval pathway. Put the blade in with straight arms, bend them as you draw the blade through so that your oar handle comes in to the base of the ribs, drop the hands to lift the blade clear of the water and straighten the arms again ready for the next stroke.

Next you will learn how to feather the blade when it is out of the water. This means turning the oar handle with your inside hand so that the back of the blade becomes parallel to the surface of the water. This is done to cut down the air resistance on the blade when you are rowing, but once you have feathered the blade you will have to square it again for the next stroke.

A squared blade

While you are learning to do this you must try all the time to make your movements as smooth as possible, and while you will have to think quite hard about them at first they will soon become quite natural and easy. Gradually you will progress to using the sliding seat, when you will find that you will get a longer stroke, but you must still think about making the blade follow an oval pathway.

A feathered blade

Using the slide brings new problems to be overcome. Unless your oar handle clears your knees first as you slide forward you will knock them. So before you start to move your slide you will have to reach forward with your body. Try to make your slide speed constant; therefore your hand speed must be constant to keep your blade moving. You must try not to crash into the frontstop or to lurch forwards at the frontstop, and you must try to keep in time with the other members of your crew.

You will also discover that when you start sliding the boat will become more difficult to balance, and only practice in blade and slide control will solve this problem for you. Your rate of progress will obviously depend upon your ability but in general the younger you are the faster you will learn, provided you can concentrate on what you are doing.

When you have learnt how to square and feather the blade, and how to row a longer stroke by using the sliding seat you should graduate to the racing boat. It will help if two beginners can go out with some slightly more experienced oarsmen as this will help you get the feeling of the movement of the boat. You should practise the whole stroke in pairs while the rest of the crew keep the boat level, and gradually the whole crew will start to row together. You might find it difficult at first to keep in time with the other members of the crew. Here again practice is the answer as you get used to the rhythm of the stroke and the movement of the boat.

Once in a crew you will have to learn the basic rowing orders which the coxswain will call out.

1. 'Easy all'	meaning	Stop rowing, blades feathered, boat balanced.
2. 'Drop'	,,	Lower the blades flat on the water.
3. 'Hold her'	,,	Stop rowing and hold the blades in the water at a slight angle, gradually turning them square in the water to stop the boat quickly.
4. 'Back her down'	,,	Turn the blades to a reversed square position in the water and row backwards.
5. 'Spin her'	,,	One side of the boat takes normal strokes, the other side 'backs her' to turn the boat round.
6. 'Back stops'	,,	The whole crew takes up the finish position of the stroke and waits for further orders.

You should also experience rowing on both sides of the boat. It will certainly be to your advantage when crews are eventually selected if you can row on either bowside or strokeside.

DISCIPLINE IN THE BOAT

There are some basic rules of behaviour in a boat to be observed by everyone for the sake of themselves, the rest of the crew, and the equipment. Remember that the equipment is expensive and difficult to replace, so you must look after it, and in the event of any danger act quickly and decisively—people cannot be replaced.

1. During practice in the boat you ought not to talk unless you are questioned by your coach or the coxswain. If you are talking while you are rowing you are obviously not thinking about what you are doing.

2. Do not watch your own blade all the time unless you are asked to. You should look at it from time to time to make sure it is doing the right things, but in the main you should look towards the stern or at stroke's blade to help you with your timing.

3. You must always keep at least one hand on the oar handle when you have stopped rowing to keep the boat stable, preferably the inside one.

4. The crew is numbered from the bows (bow, 2, 3, . . . 7, stroke, cox). You must know your number.

5. You must react immediately you are given an order.

6. If the coxswain sees an emergency approaching he must take immediate steps and not wait for the coach to tell him. The coach may not have seen it.

Cambridge University in training for the Boat Race

SOME RECOMMENDED EXERCISES FOR BEGINNERS

1. Rowing with squared blades.
2. Alternately rowing with squared and feathered blades.
3. Rowing single strokes, or a series of 2, 3, 4, or 5 strokes, stopping with the hands dropped down and pushed away so that the blade is at right angles to the boat.
4. Keeping the boat level while the blades 'row' through the air rather than the water.
5. Keeping the boat level in the 'easy' position longer than usual with the blades feathered and clear of the water.
6. Rowing with the inside hand only.
7. Rowing with the outside hand only.
8. Rowing without using the slide.
9. Using $\frac{1}{4}$, $\frac{1}{2}$, or $\frac{3}{4}$ length of slide.
10. Rowing at a very low rate of strokes.
11. Changing the rate of strokes without any orders being given.
12. Bow four rowing. Stern four sit the boat level.

All these exercises will improve your stroke and give you better control of your blade and boat. You must not forget that whatever exercise you are doing your stroke should still be a continuous, flowing motion. If you manage to do this you will rapidly gain in confidence and skill.

The most important aspect of the rowing stroke which you as a beginner must master is your timing of the blade into the water. You must use sight, sound and feel for this, and think ahead so that you are able to co-ordinate your whole body into the perfect timing of the blade. The person who is learning to coach himself shows most improvement in this field.

Rowing with inside hand only

THE ROWING STROKE

You must understand that the whole stroke is a continuous and flowing movement with the maximum of effort being directed in the water. You must always be aware of what your blade is doing and you should not be discouraged from looking at it occasionally. Do not become too obsessed about your body position but always consider the blade first. Every stroke must be your best and you must, therefore, think about every stroke. If you continue to row badly you will become mentally and physically lazy.

It is very difficult to describe a continuous cycle of movement, but the following points should help you with your basic technique of the whole stroke.

1. At the finish you should sit up, keep pressure from your legs firmly on the stretcher, and row the oar handle round, down and away from your body at the same speed as it came in.

2. Keep the blade feathered high and do not allow your slide to come forward until your hands have cleared your knees. Stretch out and do not drop your head when reaching forward, and aim for a uniform speed of slide.

3. Square the blade in good time so that you are sliding the last part forward with your blade fully squared, and gradually bring it down to the water.

4. Spring the blade into the water by a quick co-ordinated body and leg action. This is achieved by an opening of the angle between body and thighs as well as by the spring from the legs.

5. Accelerate the blade through the water. Feel as if you are hanging all your weight on the oar handle.

Maintain the leg drive to the finish and draw the outside arm hard past the body.

6. Extract the blade square and as smoothly as possible with the feet maintaining pressure on the stretcher. Feather the blade as the handle is rowed round, down and away from the body.

Let your hands clear the knees before your slide comes forward. The person rowing at No. 2 is out of phase with the rest of the crew.

The Rowing Stroke Cycle

1

2

3

4

5

Bladework

The blade is extracted by striking the oar handle down at the finish. It is then feathered as the hands move away. To begin with you should lightly touch the saxboard with the handle as the hands pass over the knees so that you learn to keep the blade feathered high off the water. As you reach half way forward on your slide start to square the blade and bring it down to the water as your body compresses at the frontstop in readiness for the beginning of the next stroke. Beginners are often very careless about their bladework and you will need to remind yourself all the time of what your blade is doing, especially on the last little bit of the forward movement. Remember—STRIKE DOWN . . . FEATHER HIGH . . . SQUARE IN GOOD TIME . . . BRING IT DOWN TO THE WATER.

The Hands

The outside hand should be at the end of the oar handle, the inside hand just on its own side of the middle of the chest. You can increase this distance to make it more comfortable for you. Both thumbs must be underneath the oar handle and the little finger of the outside hand should NOT be over the end of the handle. The outside hand acts as a hook with which to draw the blade through the water. The inside hand feathers and squares the blade with the minimum of wrist movement. When feathering, the blade handle should be rolled with the fingers and thumb of the inside hand so that it rotates inside the outside hand. When square the handle is rolled into the base of the fingers. Make sure that when you take the beginning of the stroke your outside hand is hooked round the oar handle. If it is not you may over-reach and take the beginning with the inside hand.

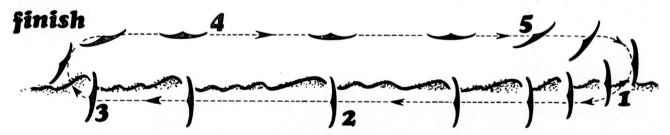

movement of blade during stroke

The Beginning

As you gather yourself on to the frontstop you must feel relaxed and ready to reverse your whole action with one spring. Do not have your knees splayed wide apart or close together, but let them take up a natural and comfortable position. As you stretch out and slide forward try to feel as if you are closing your chest up towards the thigh nearest your oar. The blade must be brought down to the water, and it should be slightly pitched forward (slightly oversquared). The arms must be straight but not stiff and as you spring in one co-ordinated body and leg movement you must feel the main weight being taken with the outside arm. Try not to develop a bent arm beginning. Your timing of the beginning is all-important and it is probably better to concentrate first on the speed and co-ordination of the movement than on the firmness of it. Practice makes perfect, and if you have a rowing tank or bank-tub you should practise this beginning until you have it right.

The finish

The blade must be accelerated through the water. The body and legs should be used together so that you feel your whole weight suspended between the stretcher and the oar handle. Watch the water building up at the front of your blade as you accelerate it and feel you are hanging your weight on the blade at the finish. Do not rush the finish or tear the blade out too early. Draw your outside arm past the body and sit in a firm open position to feel the boat being sent away from you as your oar handle is rowed round, down and away from you. Do not stop your hands at the finish, but keep them moving away at the same speed as they came in.

Throughout the stroke emphasise the leg drive. The legs are the strongest limbs of the whole body and their contribution to the stroke is all-important. Keep your back at its full height during the stroke and keep it firm, otherwise you will not co-ordinate the leg and body action and your legs will go down too early. This means that most of the power will be lost.

The Recovery Between Strokes

As the hands lead the body forward on the slide you must keep pressing the button against the gate by light pressure from the inside hand. On the forward swing of the body the hands must clear the knees before the slide starts to move, and you must feel that your hands are leading you forward to the frontstop. Slide at an even speed and as you gather yourself for the next stroke bring the blade down to the water square. Do not over-reach. This will cause you to drop your shoulders and your blade will go up in the air. Reach only as far as your strong point, so think about reaching *forward* with your shoulders and *not down*. Keep your head up and feel yourself compressed over the frontstop, ready to spring.

The Skulling Stroke Cycle

1

2

3

4

5

The Rhythm of the Strokes

The continuous cycle of movement must have a rhythm. As the maximum of effort takes place when the blades are in the water the time spent in the water will be shorter than when they are out. Try to make the power stroke one third of the whole cycle when you are practising. Keep the hands moving at the finish, and as the hands lead you forward feel relaxed and in control of your boat and blade. Do not rush up the slide but feel the speed of the boat moving underneath you rather than you moving in the boat. Your movement therefore is determined by the speed of the boat, which in turn is determined by the amount of power you apply to the blade. You must not try to force the boat to go faster by sliding faster forward on your seat. The boat will only go faster if you apply more power.

Always think ahead, and try to keep your blade moving through an oval pathway. As the boat moves horizontally through the water you must keep all vertical movements down to an absolute minimum otherwise you will 'bounce' the boat. This means that your movements and those of your blade must be as smooth as possible.

SCULLING

Many people believe that your standard of rowing can be very much improved by your ability to scull. In terms of boat control and confidence this is true, but the best scullers do not necessarily make the best members of a rowing crew. Nevertheless you should be able to scull, and for the beginner it provides an exciting challenge and a suitable alternative in mastering the basic technique of blade control and boat movement.

Beginners at sculling are quite likely to fall in and it is important that you are closely supervised. You must be able to swim and know what do do in the case of a capsize.

Putting the sculls in to the gates

Stepping into a sculling boat

And sitting down

To begin with your technique should be kept to a bare minimum—in fact all that is necessary to stay afloat. You should practise keeping the boat level with the two sculls flat on the water, and learn how the boat rolls by lifting and lowering one scull handle at a time. You will soon be left in no doubt that the first major problem you will have to overcome is one of balance. You will feel that you are on a tight-rope with your sculls acting as balancing poles, but really learning to scull is not much harder than learning to ride a bicycle.

You should try sitting at the backstop and taking a stroke with one scull at a time, before using them both together. They must not go deeper than the blade itself and they must remain at this depth during the stroke. Try very hard not to let the water run up the looms. This is very wasteful and causes drag to the speed of the boat. The blades must accelerate during the stroke and should be extracted cleanly when the stroke is completed. You will soon become aware that any mistakes you make with your sculls will be instantly felt in the balance of the boat. Nevertheless you should learn as soon as possible to keep the pressure on the sculls right to the finish by drawing the scull handles into your body. When the sculls almost touch the body at the level of the hips, the pressure stops, the hands are dropped, the shoulders relax and·the sculls come clear of the water. They are feathered by rolling the scull handle from the base of the fingers into the fingers themselves.

The sculls are held loosely and are lightly pressed out against the gates. The thumbs should be kept on the ends of the scull handles. The fact that you have two sculls as opposed to one oar in rowing means that during the stroke the handles must cross. This creates a special problem for the sculler and you must decide whether to cross your hands one above the other or one in front of the other. Most coaches now recommend that one hand should be slightly in front of the other. In this way your boat is more certain to go along level as both blades work on the same plane and at the same depth in the water, provided that the heights of your gates have also been set level. It is more common for scullers to lead with their left hand during the stroke with the right one coming in slightly after it. It is very important not to alter this relationship of the hands during the recovery, and therefor in this case it is the right hand which should lead out first in the recovery.

During the recovery you must aim to balance the boat so that neither scull touches the water as you slide for ward. As in rowing the hands must pass over the knees before the slide starts to move forward, and you mus sit up to gain the advantage of your natural height rather than slump forward. Do not stop the movement of your hands as they come round the turn and try to keep your speed of slide uniform.

As you gather yourself at the frontstop you should square the blades early by rolling the scull handles into the base of the fingers. The wrists may be slightly arched, the arms straight but not stiff. The blades must come down to the water and enter it quickly and smoothly and both together. There should be the same co-ordinated leg and body action as in rowing to ensure that you make the best use of your available power. Make sure you are in a

strong position at the frontstop with your shins vertical, and that as the sculls·enter the water the main leg drive is transmitted through your firm back and straight arms on to the sculls.

Balancing the boat

Just before the beginning

The beginning

The finish

The recovery

To scull well you will need plenty of practice and a lot of concentration on your technique. You will also find that it can be fun and often a welcome break from rowing in the eight or four. Being on your own in a sculling boat means there is no one else to upset the run of things except yourself and it is therefore a very real personal challenge to be in control of your blades and your boat.

The same basic rules apply to sculling as to rowing. If anything, in sculling, the effect of any breach of these principles is felt more drastically than in a bigger boat. Therefore you must learn how to control the blades in order to propel the boat well.

There is a lot of variety in the way the top scullers race, often because sculling technique makes the best use of what power you have available. Different scullers therefore scull in such a way as to take advantage of their different physical qualities. You should try not to copy the World Champion's style of sculling. You will develop your own style. But what you should try to copy from the World Champion is the technique of good bladework. In double and quadruple sculling, however, it is helpful to you if your way of sculling is the same as your partner's or partners' particularly in regard to sculling left hand in front of right. The machine-like precision of doing everything together is just as important in double and quadruple sculling as it is in rowing.

Two ways of carrying a sculling boat

COXING

The cox of a crew is a very important person, but one who is often taken for granted. Very few coaches take the trouble to teach their coxswains properly and therefore they often learn the hard way, sometimes to the cost of their crew or their equipment. It is worth knowing that a good coxswain will often win races for a crew, but a good crew may lose a race through bad coxing.

Every coxswain should take every opportunity to row or scull so as to be aware of the crew's problems and, like the other members of the crew, should be able to swim. It is possible to cox in a life jacket, but it could easily prove to be a hindrance to the job. A cox should be alert and intelligent; be a good judge of speeds and distances; know what to say and when to say it; be decisive; be willing to be of service and willing to learn; and be of light weight.

Take every precaution in the winter time to stay warm and dry.

Steering

First of all you must be comfortable in the boat. You are well advised to have some padding with you to place at the base of your spine or you will get a badly bruised back. Set the toggles on the two rudder lines level and hold them just in front of your hips on the saxboard between your

The coxswain

The coxswain in action

thumb and forefinger. You must sit still and brace your feet in the bottom of the boat. You must also sit up to see where you are going. If you find it difficult to steer straight try to steer on a point fixed in the distance. When you know a particular piece of river you can often steer by judging your distance from one or the other bank. You should hold the rudder lines taut but use them gently to steer round bends. Try to apply the rudder only when the blades are in the water. You will certainly tend to oversteer at first and have to apply the rudder in the opposite direction to get the boat on its proper course again. Boats pivot round a point in front of the rudder, so remember that when the bow moves in one direction the stern moves in the other. This movement is most noticeable in eights. It takes a boat a little time to respond to the rudder so you will have to anticipate bends by applying the rudder before you reach them and stop applying it before you come out. Only experience will teach you how much rudder to use and when to use it, but remember that the more you use the rudder the more effect it will have on slowing down the boat. Remember also that the shortest distance between two points is not always the quickest. The current, the wind and the water conditions all have to be taken into account. The coxswain is the only person in the boat who can really see what is happening ahead and you must tell your crew of any changes in wind or water conditions, or even obstacles in the water, so that they know what to expect. You might be able to steer to avoid the worst of it. In the event of any danger you must be quick in coming to a decision. When in serious doubt, stop!

Coaching and Encouraging

The coxswain is the coach's mouthpiece in the boat and it is important that you assist your coach occasionally by reminding the crew of any particular point that is being put across. From your seat in the stern you are also in an excellent position to watch the bladework of your crew, and a gentle reminder to a crew member to correct something can be very valuable.

You must aim to gain the confidence of your crew as quickly as possible by being decisive in the orders you give and in the actions you take. You will soon learn by your mistakes if you dither about with instructions. Your orders must be clear, short and simple. Too much talk when your crew is rowing is irritating and they will tend not to listen. Some boats have battery-powered loud-speaker systems for coxswains to use, but most have to rely on their own voice being heard by the whole crew.

The wrong method of shouting will quickly ruin your voice, so you must learn to 'sing' your words and direct them towards the bow of the boat so that everyone hears you. When giving routine orders you should give them in the rhythm of the stroke, but reminders and encouragement are best given during the relatively quiet period of the stroke when the blades are out of the water.

Try to gain every legitimate advantage you possibly can for your crew, so be alert. When you race keep your crew informed of the progress you are making, together with any information about the progress of your opposition. Your encouragement and the crew's response to it should leave you feeling as tired as they do at the end of a race.

Be sure you thoroughly know the Rules of Racing and any special rules for the race in which you are taking part. Have a good look over the course beforehand, even if you know it, because you must know the wind and water conditions of the day.

Other Duties

A coxswain must work closely with the coach, but at the same time you are part of a crew and must be involved with the rowing as much as your crew. You must therefore see that the small but important things on and off the water are carried out properly. For instance you must make sure that the boat is lifted off the rack in the boathouse properly and that on its way to the water it does not hit anything. You are just as responsible for steering the boat when it is on land as when it is on the water, and you must be prepared to lend a hand when necessary, and not just walk alongside the crew. When it is returned to the boathouse you will probably have to wash it down and leather it off. Before going afloat you will have to make sure that the oars are ready for the crew, and of course you will have to check your own steering gear.

You should try to get your crew afloat with the minimum of delay and help them to embark by keeping the boat steady as they get in. Before you step in make sure that no one in the boat needs anything. Once the boat has been pushed off from the landing stage make yourself comfortable, keep to the agreed system of giving orders and do not waste the crew's time or effort on the water. If you meet a heavy swell or wash approaching from the side and which you think might swamp the boat the safest course is to stop the boat and order the crew to raise that side of the boat by lifting their oar handles. By saying 'EASY ALL . . . HANDS UP BOWSIDE (or strokeside)' both you and your crew should remain dry.

Most coxed boats are steered by the coxswain sitting in the stern, but some are steered by coxswains lying down in the bow. Obviously this is not a very suitable place from which to give orders or to observe the crew's bladework, but it is a better position for steering as there is nothing to block your view. In boats with a prone coxswain in the bow there are no toggles to hold but the rudder lines are controlled by a pivoting lever held in one hand.

Some Orders Given by the Coxswain

1. Getting the boat afloat.
   - (i) HANDS ON . . . READY . . . LIFT
   - (ii) HALF TURN . . . WAIST HEIGHT . . . LOWER
   - (iii) SWING THE BOW TOWARDS a suitable landmark, e.g. THE BRIDGE
   - (iv) TOWARDS THE WATER . . . TURN (means turn the bottom of the boat towards the water)
   - (v) HOLD HER BOWSIDE (or strokeside) . . . STROKESIDE UNDER.
- OR (vi) THROWING HER UP . . . BOWSIDE (or strokeside) MOVING . . . READY . . . UP . . . LOWER.
   - (vii) WALK HER OUT . . . DOWN . . . LEVEL.

2. Getting the crew in.
   (i) HOLD THE BOAT BOWSIDE (or strokeside)
   (ii) STROKESIDE . . . HANDS ACROSS . . . ONE FOOT IN . . . TOGETHER.
   (iii) BLADES OUT STROKESIDE
   (iv) BOWSIDE . . . HANDS ACROSS . . . ONE FOOT IN . . . TOGETHER
   (Cox steps in last)

Hold the boat stroke-side, etc.

3. Afloat.
   (i) BACKSTOPS . . . HALF PRESSURE PADDLING . . . READY . . . GO
   (ii) NEXT STROKE . . . FULL PRESSURE
   (iii) NEXT STROKE . . . PADDLE LIGHT
   (iv) EASY ALL . . . DROP (means lower the blades on to the water)

4. Turning the boat
   (i) PADDLE ON BOWSIDE (or strokeside)
   (ii) BACK HER DOWN STROKESIDE (or bowside)

5. Coming in to the landing stage.
   (i) EASY ALL
   (ii) TURN THE BLADES OVER BOWSIDE (or strokeside)
   (Cox steps out first)
   (iii) BOWSIDE . . . HANDS ACROSS . . . ONE FOOT OUT . . . TOGETHER.
   (iv) HOLD THE BOAT BOWSIDE
   (v) BLADES OUT STROKESIDE
   (vi) STROKESIDE . . . HANDS ACROSS . . . ONE FOOT OUT . . . TOGETHER.

6. Lifting the boat out.
   (i) HANDS ON . . . READY . . . LIFT
   (ii) HOLD HER BOWSIDE (or strokeside). STROKESIDE UNDER
   (iii) TOWARDS THE WATER . . . TURN
   . . . and carry the boat back to the boathouse.

RACING

Having spent some time learning the technique of rowing you should naturally feel that you want to race somebody. It may be that your first race will be a friendly fixture against a neighbouring club or school rather than in an open regatta, but make sure that before you start racing you get your technique right.

Regattas

All open rowing competition takes place at regattas. Originally these were very grand social occasions known as water festivals where numerous water activities took place. Gradually many of these activities disappeared so that today we are mainly left with just rowing regattas. Henley Royal Regatta is the most famous regatta in this country and still holds a special place in the rowing and social calendar. For many people who row an appearance at Henley is a very significant milestone in their rowing career. Apart from our own schools, colleges, universities and clubs the regatta regularly attracts a very large overseas entry every year.

The regatta season is mainly between May and the end of August. You are sure to find at least one regatta being run every weekend during that time. Sometimes a number may be held on the same day in different parts of the country. The racing is usually on a knock-out basis, two crews racing abreast, with the winners progressing through the heats to the final. Racing often lasts all day if there are a large number of events, and every regatta is well supported and provides the competitors with very keen and enjoyable racing. There are many 'pots' and trophies to be won at the end of the day.

Most of our regattas are run in this way, but in many International and Championship events races are held on multi-lane courses with up to 6 boats racing at the same time. The standard international distances are 2000 metres for men, 1500 metres for Juniors and 1000 metres for women. Multi-lane racing allows a system of racing known as repechage where the losers of the first heats race each other again to ensure that the fastest crews go on to the semi-finals and the finals.

Racing at Henley Royal Regatta

Multi-lane racing, Olympic Games **1972**

Racing Classification

Most regattas offer events for everyone from the beginner to the senior. Basically your classification in rowing is determined first by your age and then by the number of wins you have. Up to the age of 18 you may compete as a Junior, but you are not restricted just to Junior events. Nevertheless there is plenty of racing available to the Junior ranging from events at under 14, 15 and 16 level to Junior B and Junior A.

If you are over 18 years of age you are a Senior and must compete in Senior events, although Juniors may also compete in them. Again there is a classification structure of Senior C, Senior B, Senior A and Elite. Progress through the different classifications is by the number of wins you have, provided that they are over a qualifying distance of not less than 1000 metres. When you win 6 qualifying races you become an Elite. The same classification rules apply to women's rowing except that the qualifying race distance is 800 metres.

A Novice event is open to anyone who has never won an open event at a regatta, and Novice events are not subject to any age limit. Sculling and rowing classifications are separate, and wins in one do not affect the other.

Veteran Rowing

If you are over 32 years of age you become a Veteran. There are various divisions for veteran rowing. ·

Lightweight events are held for crews whose average weight (excluding coxswains) must not exceed 150 lbs. (67·5 kgs.). No one entering a lightweight event may be heavier than 154 lbs. (70 kgs.), and a lightweight single sculler may not be more than 150 lbs. (67·5 kgs.). Women must not exceed 126 lbs. (55 kgs.) in their lightweight category.

Coxswains are not subject to classification, although they are subject to the age restrictions for Junior racing. They must, however, have a minimum weight—110 lbs. (50 kgs.) for Senior events, and 88 lbs. (40 kgs.) for Junior and women's events. Women may act as coxswains in men's crews and vice versa, but men and women are not allowed to row with or against each other in open events.

Head of the River Races

The long-distance races which normally take place outside the main regatta period are called Head of the River Races. Whereas summer regatta courses may take about 5 or 6 minutes to complete, a Head race can take over 20 minutes. All Head races are very well supported by crews who regard long distance rowing as the basis of their training. The races differ from regattas in so far as there is no knock-out competition. Every crew is timed separately and given a finishing time and overall position at the end of the race.

It is then a race against the clock. Each crew is started one after the other from a start line and rows to the finish line. Overtaking is of course allowed, but crews have to be

Head of the river races

careful not to baulk each other or they risk being disqualified.

Head of the River Races are very popular events and the large number of entries presents a very special problem of organisation, particularly with regard to marshalling the crews before the start, but once under way the race provides a very spectacular sight. The Head of the River Race rowed on the Tideway in London attracts over 300 eights from all over the country each year. The Schools Head regularly attracts over 150 eights and fours, the Fours Head nearly 200 entries and the Scullers Head over 300 entries. In each Head of the River Race different pennants are awarded for different categories and classifications thus providing competition throughout the whole range of age, ability and experience.

SELECTING A CREW

The first point that has to be considered when forming a crew is to decide what type of boat will produce the best results for you. There are no hard and fast rules as to whether your coach puts you in an eight, a four, or a pair. It is not just a question of deciding on the best people at the time of selection, but who will be the most effective at the time of racing. Therefore you are likely to be judged not only on your technical ability, but also on your probable rate of improvement, your physical qualities, your determination and keenness.

The only true guide to your performance is the power you produce on your blade in the water. Therefore you should be able to use your strength and your weight effectively at all times. The best way for this to be assessed is through trial races in pairs and fours where experimental combinations can be tried and changed. Only from the small units can the fastest large units be formed. Often the real problem will not be for your coach to select the crew but to convince you that the selection has been fair.

With regard to the seating in the boat certain general principles hold true. Experienced people in the stern, heavyweights in the middle and lightweights in the bow. These rules must not be followed absolutely for it is worth remembering that the true index of your merit is not your weight, height or experience, but your effectiveness in the water.

TRAINING

Having practised your technique and learnt how to use your oar effectively you should find yourself in a selected crew of some kind. The coaching you should receive now will be basically crew coaching rather than individual attention, and you will find that your crew has a purpose in being together—to try to become an effective and fast single unit. Your practice sessions will now become training outings. You will still be doing technical exercises in the boat to improve your stroke and you will have to concentrate as hard as you did when you were learning the basics, because in rowing you have to try to produce your best stroke every stroke. You may even find that from time to time your coach will take you out of the boat and back into the tank or the tub to improve some aspects of your technique that need attention.

Gradually you will find that as your crew gets more and more together and the boat begins to move more smoothly you will be covering longer distances in the course of an outing. You will learn that when you are tired you will still have to think about your bladework or the rowing will become uncomfortable instead of enjoyable. You will start to learn about higher rates of striking and how the boat moves faster as a result of harder pressure and faster blade, body and slide movements. Certainly before long you will be experiencing the feeling of the boat fizzing along underneath you even though you may not be able to keep it up for very long at a time. You will also learn that mistakes do have a habit of cropping up—if you have never heard of 'catching a crab' you will soon learn what it is when it happens to you.

Once bitten by the rowing 'bug' you will either be content to use rowing as a recreation or you will want to find greater excitement and enjoyment in competing and training for competition. Your foot will now be at the bottom of the ladder. How far up the ladder you go will depend on your desire to succeed, your ability to keep improving your rowing and the way you tackle your training.

Apart from a high level of technique there are four main physical qualities which you should aim to develop through your training for rowing:

1. Strength.
2. Endurance.
3. Speed.
4. Speed-endurance.

Strength and endurance are basically developed during the preparation period of your year's training, during the winter months. Strength is developed through weight-training and circuit-training in the gymnasium, and also through low-rate, full-pressure paddling in the boat, or by small-boat training. Endurance is developed through long-distance or long-time activities such as running and games playing or through long-distance rowing on the water.

In the competition period of the summer months the accent turns to developing speed and speed-endurance by gradually extending the pieces of rowing done with a higher rate and full pressure. Different types of interval training are used to achieve this through repeated short distances of rowing followed by rest periods. No period of training is more important than the other, but all your training must be directed towards making your boat go fast for as long as possible. This is what speed-endurance training achieves, and rowing is principally a speed-endurance sport. Therefore in the same way as you need bread and jam to make a jam sandwich so you need speed and endurance to produce rowing performance.

Every outing you have in your boat will have an aim. This may simply be a technical one to improve the blade action or the balance of the boat, but it is more usual for your aim to be directed towards improving one of the physical qualities which go into rowing training. Whether this aim is endurance or speed you should always give your best so that you come back satisfied that the aim has been achieved.

Each outing should start with a good period of warming up and then pass on to a period of technical exercises to improve your boat control. Next should come the main part of your outing where the work with its particular aim is done. Finally there should be a calming down or winding down period for recovery and relaxation.

During any part of your rowing career you should set yourself targets to achieve. At first your target may simply be to master your technique, but as you progress and start to move your boat effectively you should set your sights on competing and winning certain races. Do not set your sights too low, or the challenge of improving your performance may not be satisfying to you. A yearly improvement in your technical and physical ability should point the way to a higher standard provided that you continue to enjoy your rowing and have the mental determination to succeed.

CONCLUSION

In describing rowing, Steve Fairbairn, one of the world's most famous rowing men, wrote 'The whole sensation is one of joy and exhilaration. It is a nerve tonic which braces the whole system . . . '

Have a go! Join in

It is really very difficult to describe the attraction of rowing to someone who has never experienced it, for it is a sport which aims to get machine-like precision of timing and effort from all its participants. The individual flair of the skilful games player is swallowed up in rowing by the fact that the whole crew must strive together as one person from beginning to end. If you take up rowing, like everything else, it will need practice. All world champions are beginners at some time, but through practice and training results will come.

Rowing exists wherever there are suitable stretches of water. Don't be afraid to have a go. Your local club will be pleased to see you and will help you all they can. Go Rowing . . . Rowing is a growing sport . . . Join in!

The Amateur Rowing Association is the governing body of the sport in England and Wales. Scotland and Ireland have their own Associations. Any enquiries should be addressed to:—

The Executive Secretary
Amateur Rowing Association.
6, Lower Mall,
Hammersmith,
London W6 9DJ.   Telephone 01 748 3632/3.

Photo acknowledgements
Chris Blackwall
Dick Crane
Geoff Brook

The publishers would like to thank Mr. Barry Appleby for permission to reproduce his cartoon on page 11.

Text edited by
J. H. Page, O.B.E.

Printed by
Joseph Ward & Co. (Printers) Ltd., Wesley Place, Wellington Road, Dewsbury. Tel.: Dews. 465827 and 463502.